THE LAST RESORT

UNIVERSITY PRESS OF FLORIDA

Florida A&M University, Tallahassee
Florida Atlantic University, Boca Raton
Florida Gulf Coast University, Ft. Myers
Florida International University, Miami
Florida State University, Tallahassee
New College of Florida, Sarasota
University of Central Florida, Orlando
University of Florida, Gainesville
University of North Florida, Jacksonville
University of South Florida, Tampa
University of West Florida, Pensacola

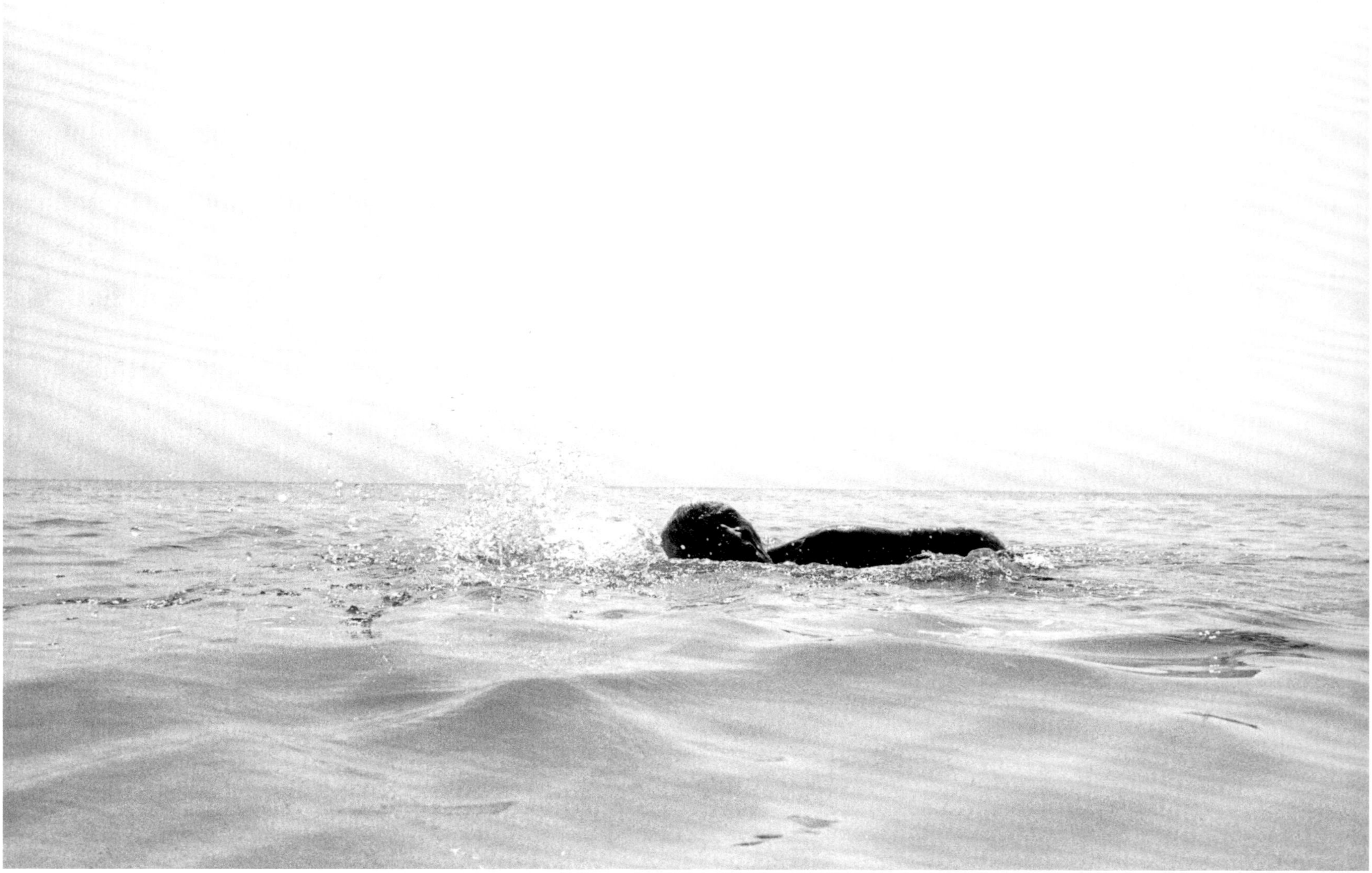

South Beach, 1980

THE LAST RESORT

Jewish South Beach, 1977–1986

Gary Monroe

UNIVERSITY PRESS OF FLORIDA

Gainesville · Tallahassee · Tampa · Boca Raton

Pensacola · Orlando · Miami · Jacksonville · Ft. Myers · Sarasota

Published in the United States of America. Printed in Canada on acid-free paper.

25 24 23 22 21 20 6 5 4 3 2 1

ISBN 978-0-8130-6652-3
Library of Congress Control Number: 2019954909

The University Press of Florida is the scholarly publishing agency for the State University System of Florida, comprising Florida A&M University, Florida Atlantic University, Florida Gulf Coast University, Florida International University, Florida State University, New College of Florida, University of Central Florida, University of Florida, University of North Florida, University of South Florida, and University of West Florida.

University Press of Florida
2046 NE Waldo Road
Suite 2100
Gainesville, FL 32609
http://upress.ufl.edu

THE LAST RESORT

Jewish South Beach, 1977–1986

THOSE OF US WHO GREW UP in Miami Beach in the 1950s and 1960s didn't quite get it. Palm trees were mops and the land was flat. We saw the sign on the MacArthur Causeway welcoming us to "America's Playground," but it meant no more to us than Jackie Gleason's tagline that the show was coming from "The Fun and Sun Capital of the World." Our world was isolated because Miami Beach was a barrier island. This was even truer for those who lived in the poorer end of the "Billion Dollar Sandbar," South Beach. We took for granted the aged Jewish population that was all around us while politicians would come to make fun of them, calling the community "God's Waiting Room" and "A Gerontological Ghetto," until they needed votes. Then they would come and sing in Yiddish at the small covered platform by the beach at Ninth Street and hand out Dixie cups of vanilla ice cream.

The Beach's glamour days waned as we were coming of age. Semblances abounded, though. A few of Carl Fisher's hotels remained but in varied stages of disrepair. My family had a cabana at the Floridian Hotel, where I photographed twenty years later. But by then it was the Biscaya, a halfway house of sorts, straight out of Fellini. The Fleetwood and the Flamingo hotels would fall during my childhood and become high-rise apartment buildings along Biscayne Bay—Forte Towers and Morton Towers, both fifteen stories of those grand tributes to modernism. Earlier on it was the bay, not the ocean, that attracted tourists. Boat races and a water-skiing elephant worked their marketing magic then, and further north, the Nautilus Hotel, taken over by the army during World War II, became Mount Sinai Hospital, where I was born in 1951.

By then activity moved beachside, and swank hotel lobbies and extravagant entertainment abounded. This wasn't necessarily the opera or even the theater crowd, but at least if it was, people shed these activities for more pedestrian shows when here, on vacation from their northern homes, often enjoying headline entertainers at the Fontainebleau, Eden Roc, Deauville, and Carillon hotels along Millionaire's Row, which stretches further northward and far away from South Beach. Scores of smaller, less opulent hotels lined Collins Avenue. The stylish Saxony, Sea Isle, and Seville filled those ranks, while still smaller hotels were lined one after the other along Ocean Drive in South Beach. Entertainment budgets changed; poolside dances, bingo games, and hot dog parties were staples the further south one stayed. Those smaller-scale hotels were well complemented by Lummus Park across the street (no development was permitted between Fifth and Fourteenth Streets) with the hundreds of coconut palm trees' bases painted white and illuminated with colored spotlights and a full moon lit a silvery ocean while its breezes swept inland.

Miami was a physically hostile frontier when Isidor Cohen settled there in early 1896. He was not the first Jewish person, but he was the first permanent resident along the shores of Biscayne Bay. He opened a dry goods store on Avenue D (which became Miami Avenue) while what would become Miami Beach was a mangrove sandbar waiting to be dredged and filled to become incorporated in 1915. A Jewish community existed on Miami Beach well before 1935, which was the year that the nucleus of Jewish presence shifted from Miami to Miami Beach, across the causeways, separated by Biscayne Bay.

The seeds for Florida, Miami Beach in particular, being the place to realize the American dream were planted from the start, and grew as soon as Henry Flagler's railroad tracks unfurled south along the east coast, reaching a fledgling Miami. Mythology grew into reality. The land was steamy and fecund, a wild place for the adventurous. After the

Second World War the image of Paradise, in the form of raising families and living full lives along endless beaches and a boundless horizon, was sensed by many of the two million soldiers and others stationed throughout the Sunshine State. There were no fences separating the enlisted and officers from civilians, and Miami Beach was unlike the rest of the United States that way and in other ways; it wasn't even like its southern neighbors and was unlike the rest of Florida in so many ways. The dredged mangrove swamp *cum* "The World's Playground" epitomized the good life in postwar America.

It wasn't always that way, and it wasn't always a mecca for Jewish people. Hoteliers' brochures announced "Gentile clientele" or "Restricted clientele." Couched terminology included "References required" and "With restrictions." Relatively few hoteliers were unwelcoming to Jews, though. The often discussed "No dogs No Jews" signs are undocumented and according to Miami Beach's historian Seth Bramson, they never existed. By the war's end initiatives were in place and laws banning anti-Semitism on Miami Beach followed. Miami Beach was becoming ever more attractive to Jews, fostering its becoming a Jewish resort and community.

In spite of city founders Carl Fisher and John Collins being, to some degree, anti-Semites, Jewish people were not deterred. They had experience with resort life in the Catskills. The Borscht Belt wintered in sunny Florida, finding comfort, camaraderie, and culture on Miami Beach, first as vacationers and then as residents. Any remnants of the gilded age gave way to a community of Jewish families. Isaac Bashevis Singer told me, America for the mass of citizens is less a melting pot than "a place to grow in their own culture, in their own way of life altered to their roots, their languages, to their hopes and wishes." In other words, immigrants came to maintain their cultural identity.

Carl Fisher's advertising of Miami Beach announced the pleasures the burgeoning city offered over living in the cold North. The Dixie Highway and the Florida East Coast Railway, both constructed long before the airlines, promoted Greater Miami, along with the obvious–sand, sun, and surf—but it was opportunity that sealed the deal. This was a place in the making, a place to make oneself anew and to do it in the tropics. Tourists proudly carried their Burdine's Department Store bag back home, to the North and the Midwest, which was a badge of distinction. Lincoln Road became known as "the Fifth Avenue of the South," while the Atlantic Ocean offered relief during the day and alcohol fueled the nightlife. Stars and personalities came to Miami Beach in the 1930s and 1940s, and afterward.

There were downturns, to be sure. In 1938 gambling was constitutionally outlawed, which crippled growth and development. The mansions lining Collins Avenue, especially north of the Eden Roc Hotel, gave way to large and impersonal condominiums and apartment houses. The flagship Fontainebleau and the few other posh hotels catered to the wealthy, while the hotels progressively southward attracted a more sedate set. Jet travel and, later, deregulation opened the skies and gave way to package vacation deals such as the American Plan. Meanwhile the many small art deco hotels and apartment buildings in South Beach became home to elderly Jews, many retiring there and some coming seasonally. Jewish families tended to live north of there, while the Beach's wealthiest lived on the tony islands of Miami Beach surrounded by Biscayne Bay.

During the late 1950s and through the mid-1960s, Miami Beach was comprised of approximately 80 percent Jewish people. That number would be increased if not for the non-Jewish strongholds of Sunset Islands 1 and 2. South Beach during the 1960s and 1970s was another kind of communal stronghold, a rarified and intriguing place where faith and lifestyles merged. Few travelers came to South Beach; it was an autonomous zone. Of course some intrepid young tourists, some surfers revisiting their youth at First Street Beach and a few others, like boxers at Fifth Street Gym, made their way to South Beach. Occasionally children visited their grandparents. But to put it mildly they were the exception. It wasn't a vacation destination. Wherever one looked, people in their 70s, 80s, and 90s populated the views. In a way it was surreal; in a way it was beautiful. It was the last leg of this historic migration, of a people who would no longer be replaced. Their children would be Americanized Jews. Still, the elderly residents' lives here weren't only sun worshipping and moonlight dances. There was also squalor and loneliness.

Those people established South Beach as the last resort, to maintain their cultural identity and live out their lives comfortably. They lived joyfully and in accord with their Old World values and religious faith until the advent of the art deco craze. South Beach was ever susceptible given that in 1980 the forces of change were coming together; the properties, fueled by the city of Miami Beach enacting a building moratorium, stifled landowners from making improvements. South Beach became depressed, and while inviting outside investors also invited the poorest to locate there, including just-arrived Marielitos.

The place soon repelled tourists. South Beach was an embarrassment to the rest of Miami Beach, and it was hardly on the map of Greater Miami. In a rush to redevelop the southern shore, the powers-that-were lost sight of something even more powerful: You don't tell Holocaust survivors that they will be "relocated." As the lack of change lingered and the deteriorating conditions worsened, blight spread. No one placed value on a refuge whose roots extended back to the shtetls (Jewish towns) of Eastern Europe.

Through the 1970s into the mid-1980s a shared vision of life went on: card rooms were transformed into makeshift temples. The ocean was therapeutic. The streets were active. Everything was within walking distance. Social agencies cared for the residents and neighbors cared for each other. On Friday evenings women lit Shabbos candles. But ever-present pushkas (tin boxes for depositing coins that would go to supporting Israel) and mezuzahs (a prayer in a small case that was affixed to doorjambs) began vanishing along with the lifestyles and mores that defined South Beach.

Meanwhile crime in Miami soared and South Beach took much of the wrath. Sunrise swims came to an abrupt end. The final blow was the airing of *Miami Vice*, which imaged Greater Miami as steamy and sexy but also a haven for crime. In a classic case of life imitating art, a television show was the catalyst for the rebirth of Miami Beach.

There was the movie *Scarface* also, which mirrored the crime-ridden aspect of Miami then, along with the newscasts of the McDuffie riots in the black ghetto of Overtown that was just over the causeway from South Beach, albeit a world away. The artist Christo's "Surrounded Islands" shined a new light on the potential of Miami as an art city, as his photographs of Biscayne Bay's spoil islands draped in shocking pink spoke of life and beauty, especially as illuminated by the tropical sun. Glamour was returning to Miami and especially to South Beach.

Attrition would have taken its toll, but the economy refused to wait. The fever to capitalize on the art deco district and get Miami Beach back into the limelight accelerated fiscal investment. New Yorkers and Europeans couldn't believe the price for land and the summer-in-winter climate. As neon lights added a cool glow to balmy nights, South Beach soon redefined "trendy," and the average age of people there dropped by about fifty years within a decade.

Front porches, where the elderly used to sit and talk about their grandchildren and Israel, became outdoor cafes while lobbies doubled as restaurants. Elderly women who had pulled "schlepping carts" during their morning chores gave way to supermodels who posed for international advertisements. Rollerbladers replaced mandolin bands along Lummus Park and croissants replaced rugeleh. But like the history of Miami, South Beach has had its ups and down during the past thirty years. Money was made and lost and the place has lost its bohemian sense of discovery to become a place of designer labels mixed with big-box stores. It's all coming to be expected: creative surprise lost to corporate homogenization.

Newcomers could not appreciate the vivacious life-affirming way that the elderly Jews began the New Year. New Year's Eve parties were thrown for their guests at just about all of the some 200 hotels along Ocean Drive and Collins Avenue. With enthusiasm, they cavorted and danced their way into a tentative future. But with each new year there were fewer and fewer celebratory parties. Morale, more than increased age, slowed them down as they saw their community withering away. The party atmosphere, as if a barometer, measured the community's demise to the point where in 1986 only three hotels held parties, and those were lackluster. The unique lifestyle of that South Beach was over as if it never happened.

South Beach has become a metaphor for everything that it wasn't. The few square miles that had given refuge to the elderly is again the "American Riviera" that attracts the young, rich, and famous. This is how it looks in selfies. Ferraris can be rented by the hour for cruising up and down Ocean Drive. Alcoholic drinks are served at outdoor cafes in goldfish bowls before noon. Yiddish became the exception and is no longer heard, while seemingly every other language is being spoken there. Costs have escalated so much that Hollywood filmmaking has pushed aside high-end photo shoots for glossy print ads. The hotels have again been transformed; even the backdrop is different: the small buildings that had formed a pedestrian community are dwarfed by neck-craning high-rises. Today all the hotels and most of the apartment buildings have either been beautifully renovated or razed. And no trace remains of the precious legacy that the elderly Jews created—a distinct and forgotten epoch.

THE LAST RESORT

Swimmers at sunrise, 1982

People congregated regularly at Tenth Street Beach to begin the morning in a therapeutic ocean. This practice ceased in 1981 as the crime rate increased, and they no longer made their way to the beach for sunrise.

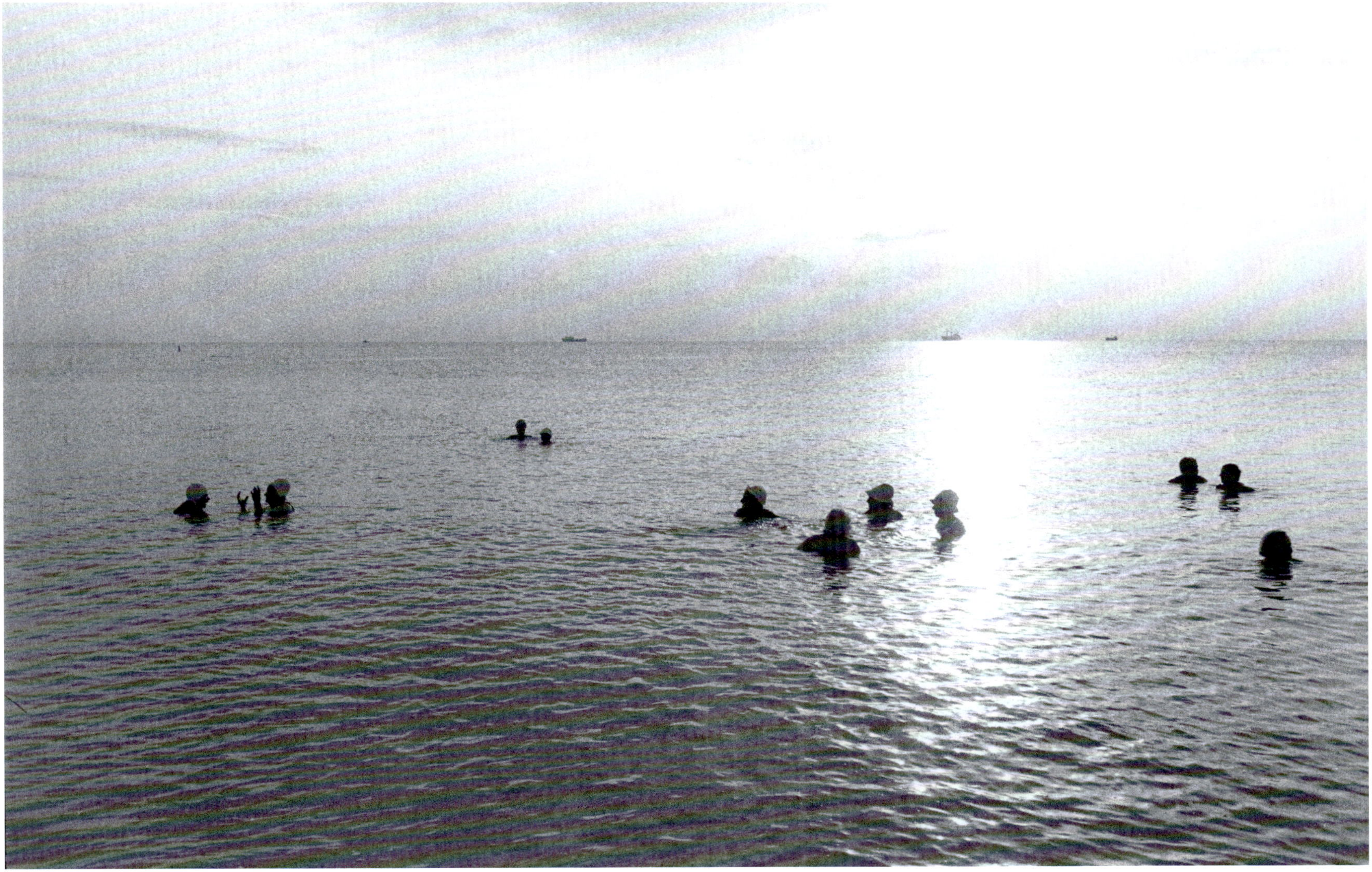

Swimmers at sunrise, 1978

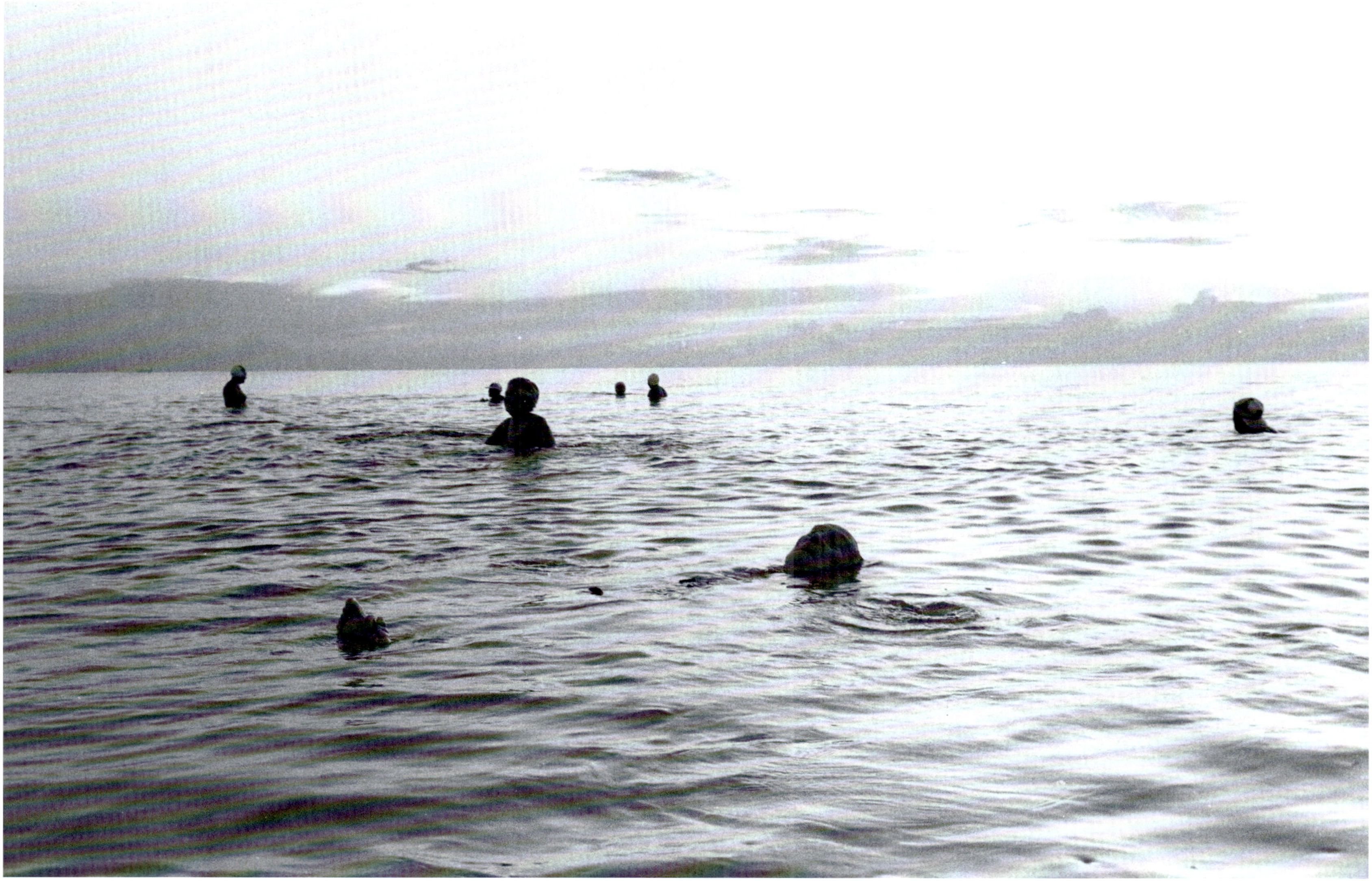

Morning prayer, 1983

There was considerable orthodoxy in South Beach. Many of the hotels along Ocean Drive, Collins Avenue, and Washington Avenue converted card rooms and social halls into makeshift shuls (synagogues) to accommodate their clienteles' needs of twice-daily prayer. The shuls are gone now, replaced by bars and restaurants.

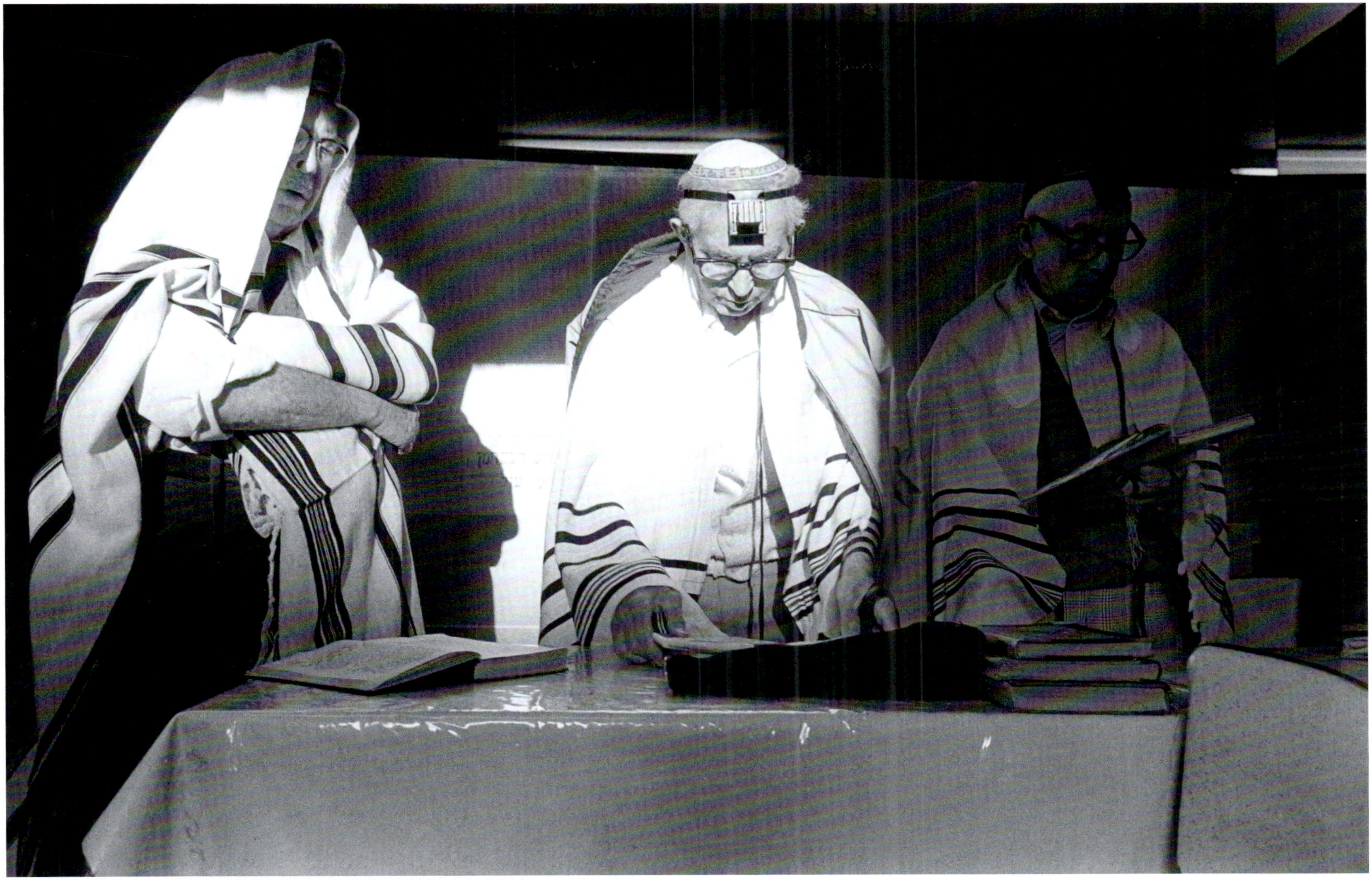

Morning prayer, 1981

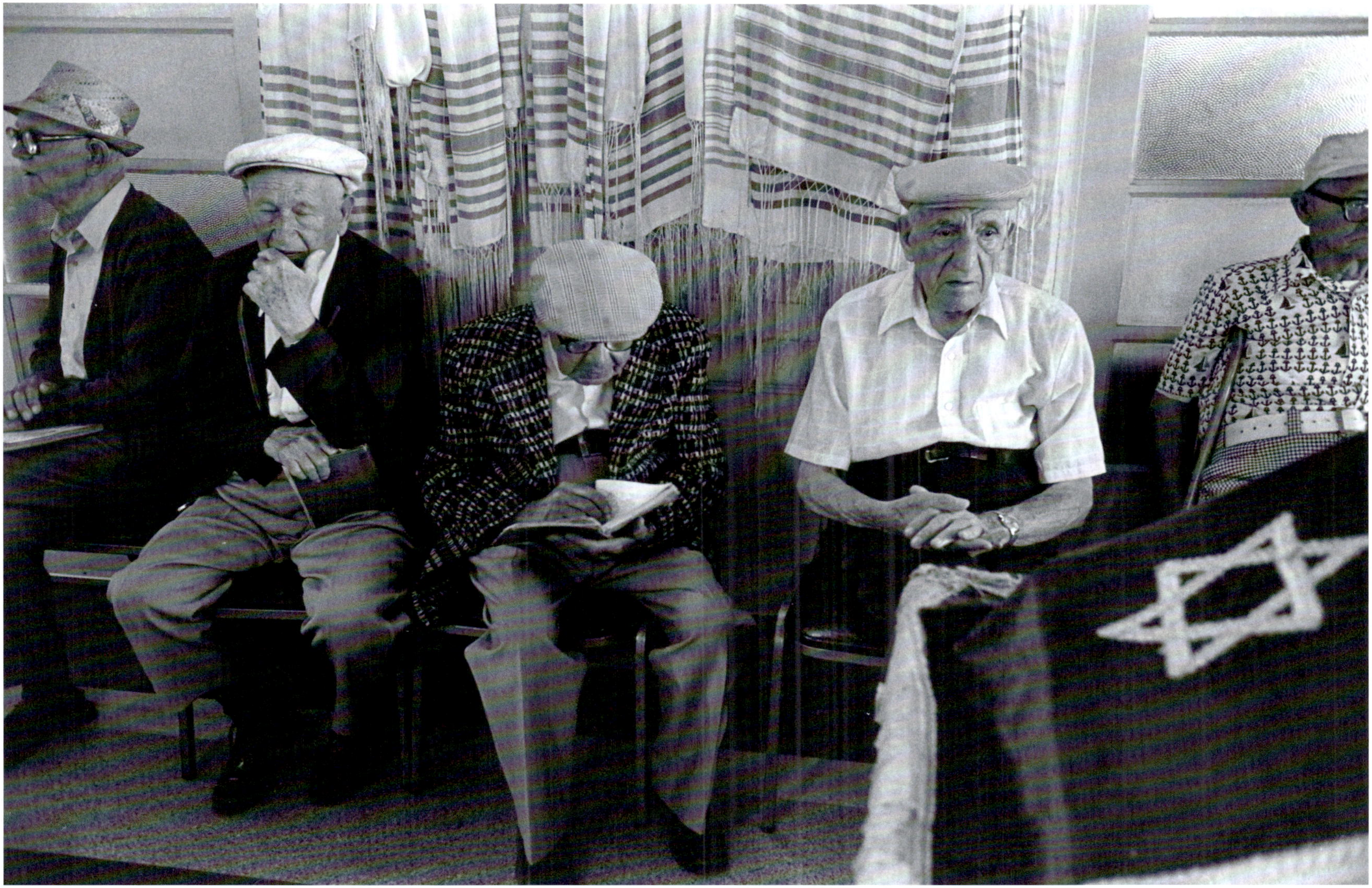

Morning prayer, 1984

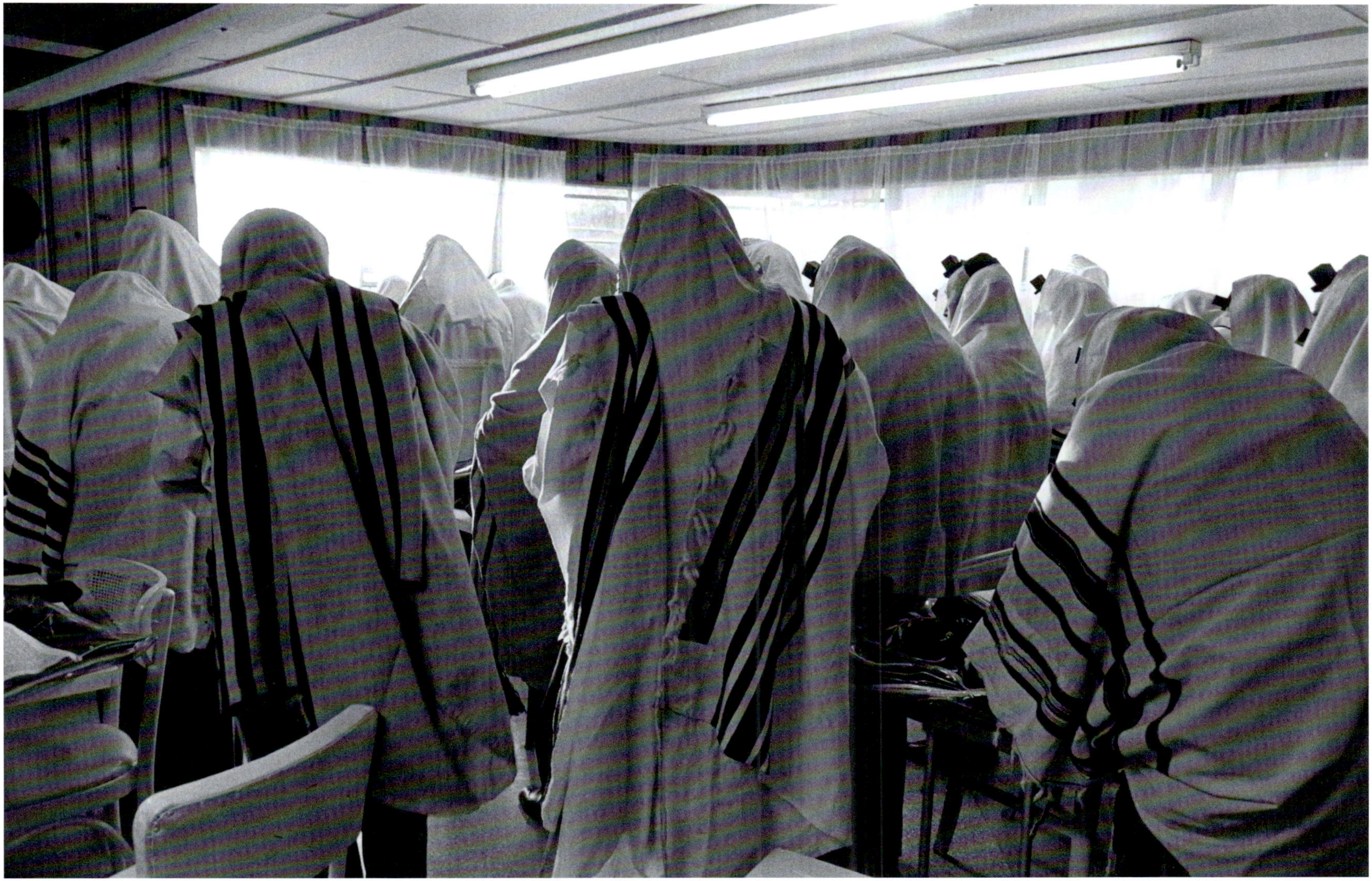

Exercise group, 1978

Exercise groups formed most mornings along Lummus Park, a strip of land that ran between the beach and Ocean Drive. Rose Silverman, who often started the session by doing a headstand, led this group, the most popular one.

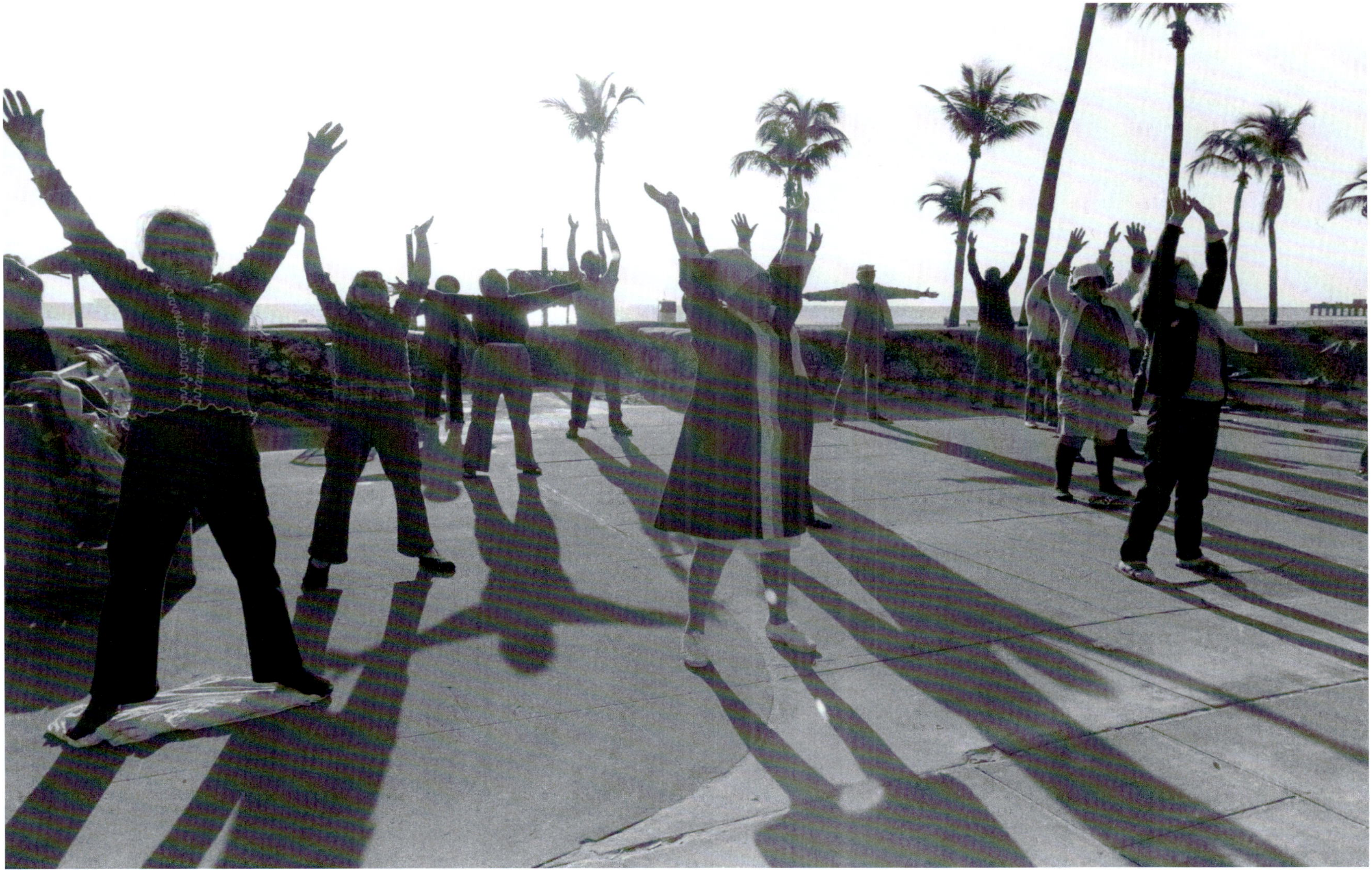

Porch sitters, 1978

Porch-sitting was a favorite pastime, particularly at the hotels along Ocean Drive because of the lovely views they offered of palm trees, sky, and ocean. These porches were wider and designed for socializing, unlike those of the hotels along Collins Avenue and Washington Avenue.

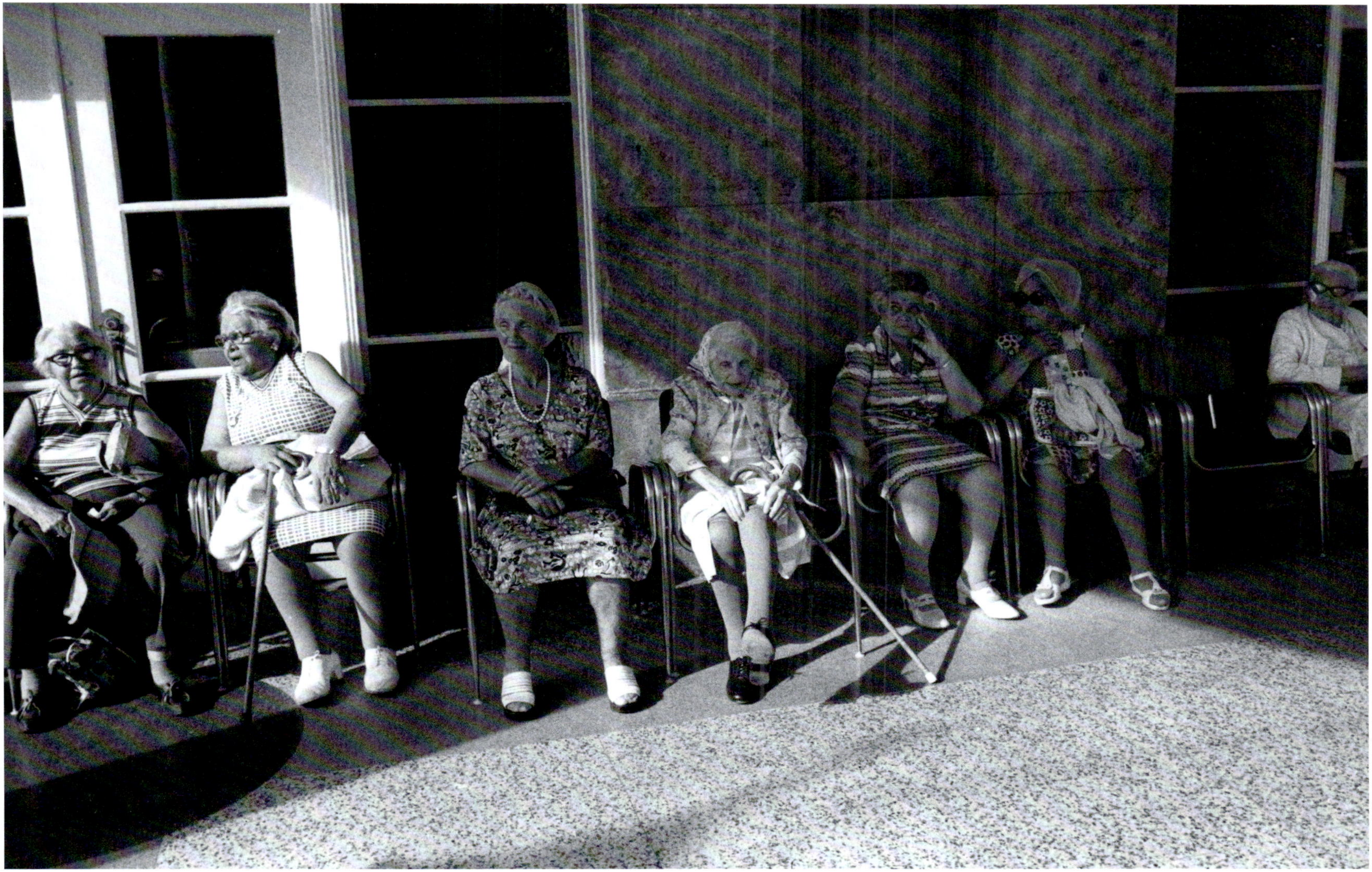

Porch sitters, 1979

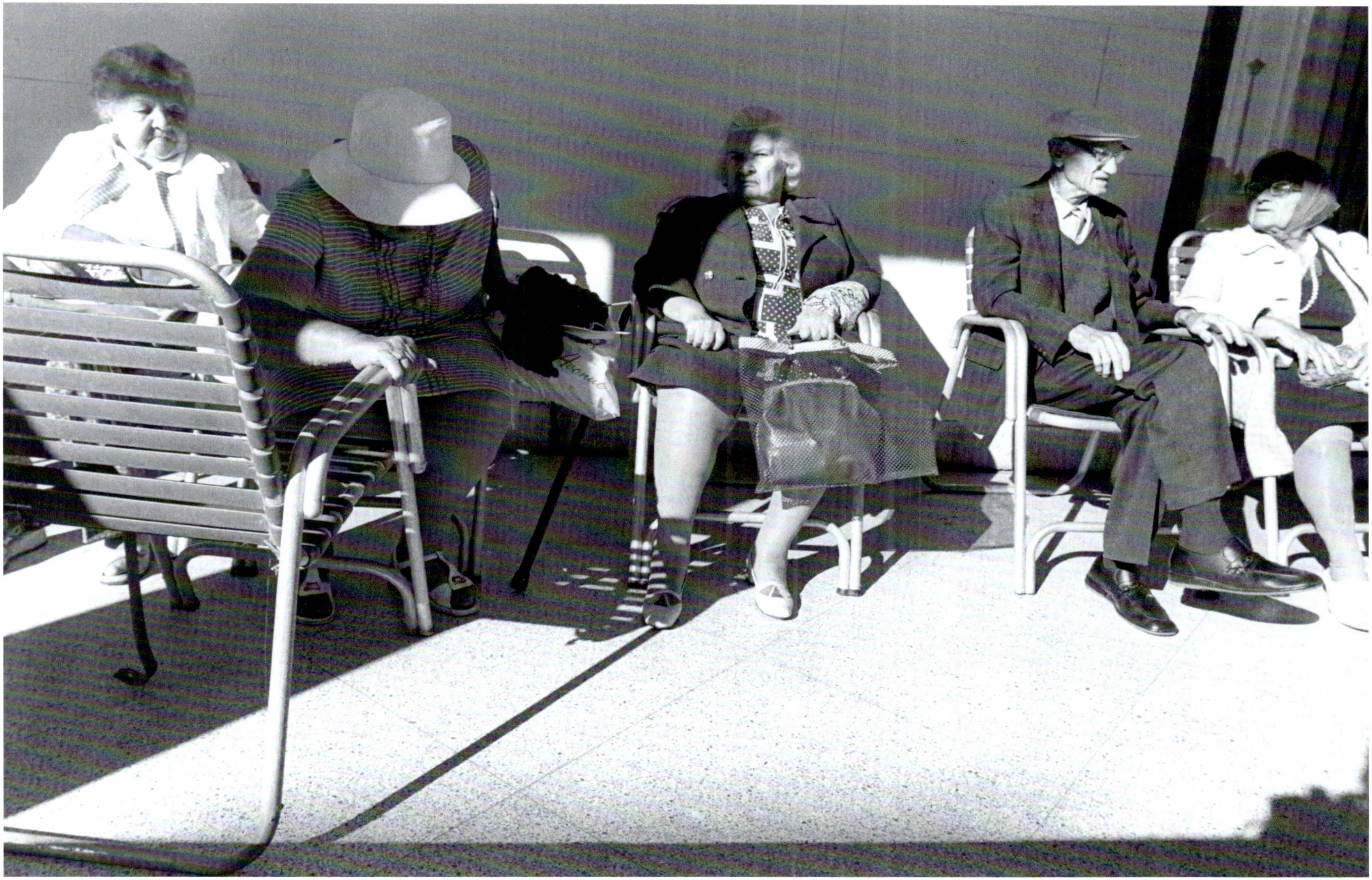

Musicians, 1978

Musicians brought their instruments to Lummus Park, attracting audiences. Gatherings of varying sizes formed for a few hours of socializing; they often sang, typically in Yiddish.

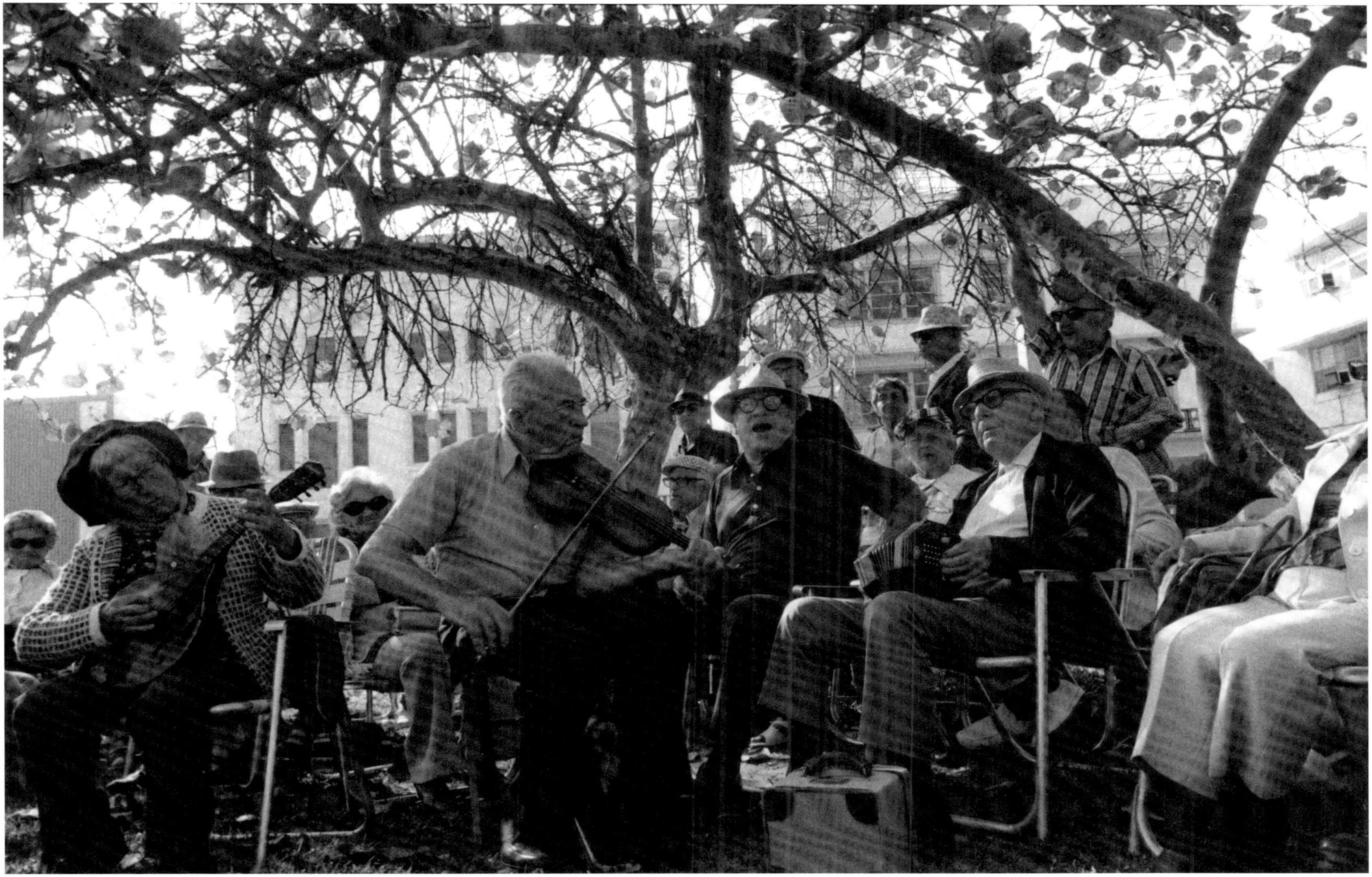

Poolside, 1979

Only three hotels among the many that line Ocean Drive (Park Central, Edison, Clevelander) had swimming pools; they were not necessary since the ocean was at their doorstep. Hotels were larger above Fifteenth Street, and these oceanfront hotels had pools and even cabanas for their guests.

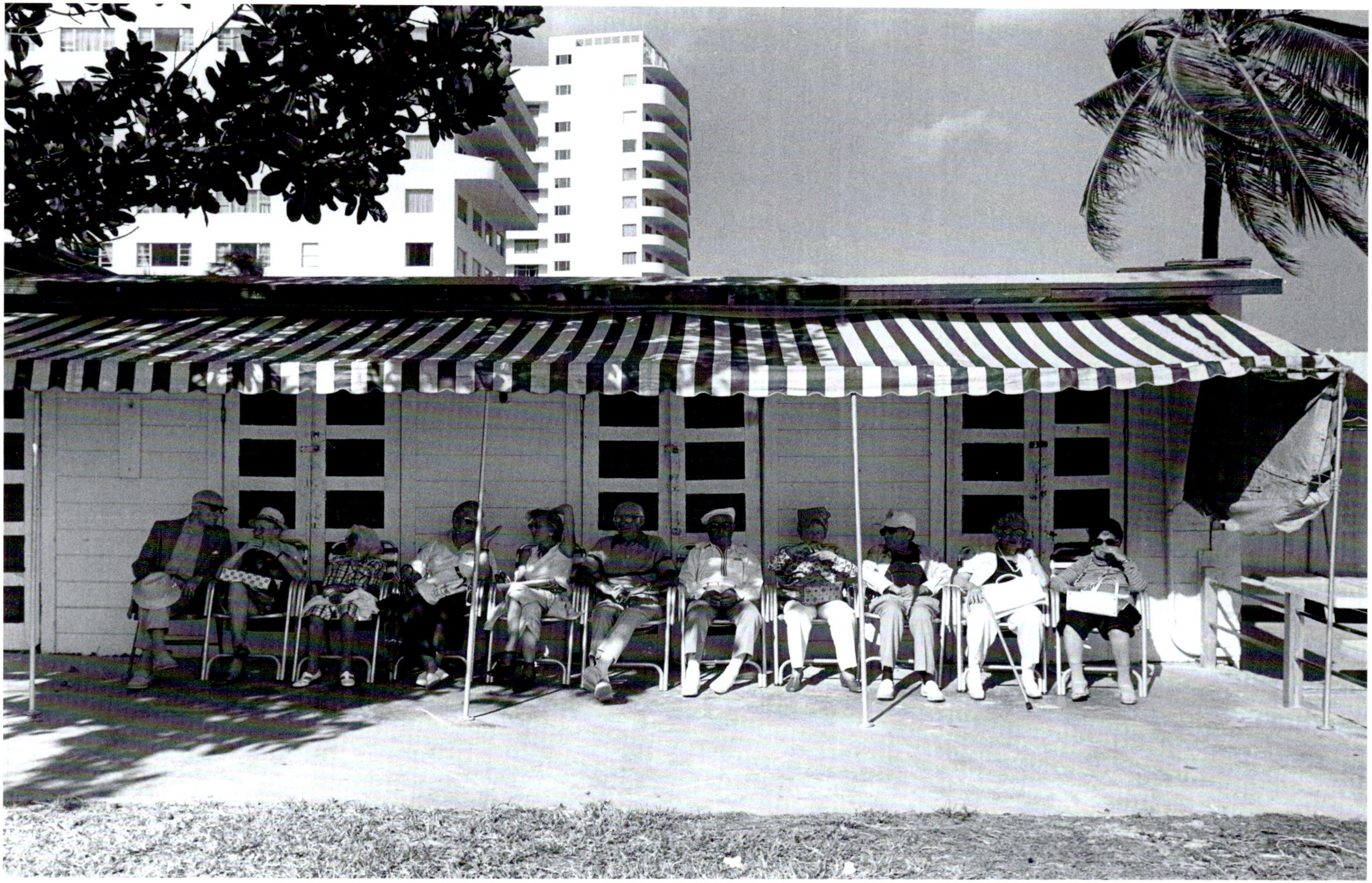

Women by calendar, 1977

Designed during the city's halcyon days, the date and temperature display was a popular place to have a snapshot taken; it also was a place to sit and rest. Sea grape leaves perched in one's mouth provided an alternative to zinc oxide for protecting lower lips.

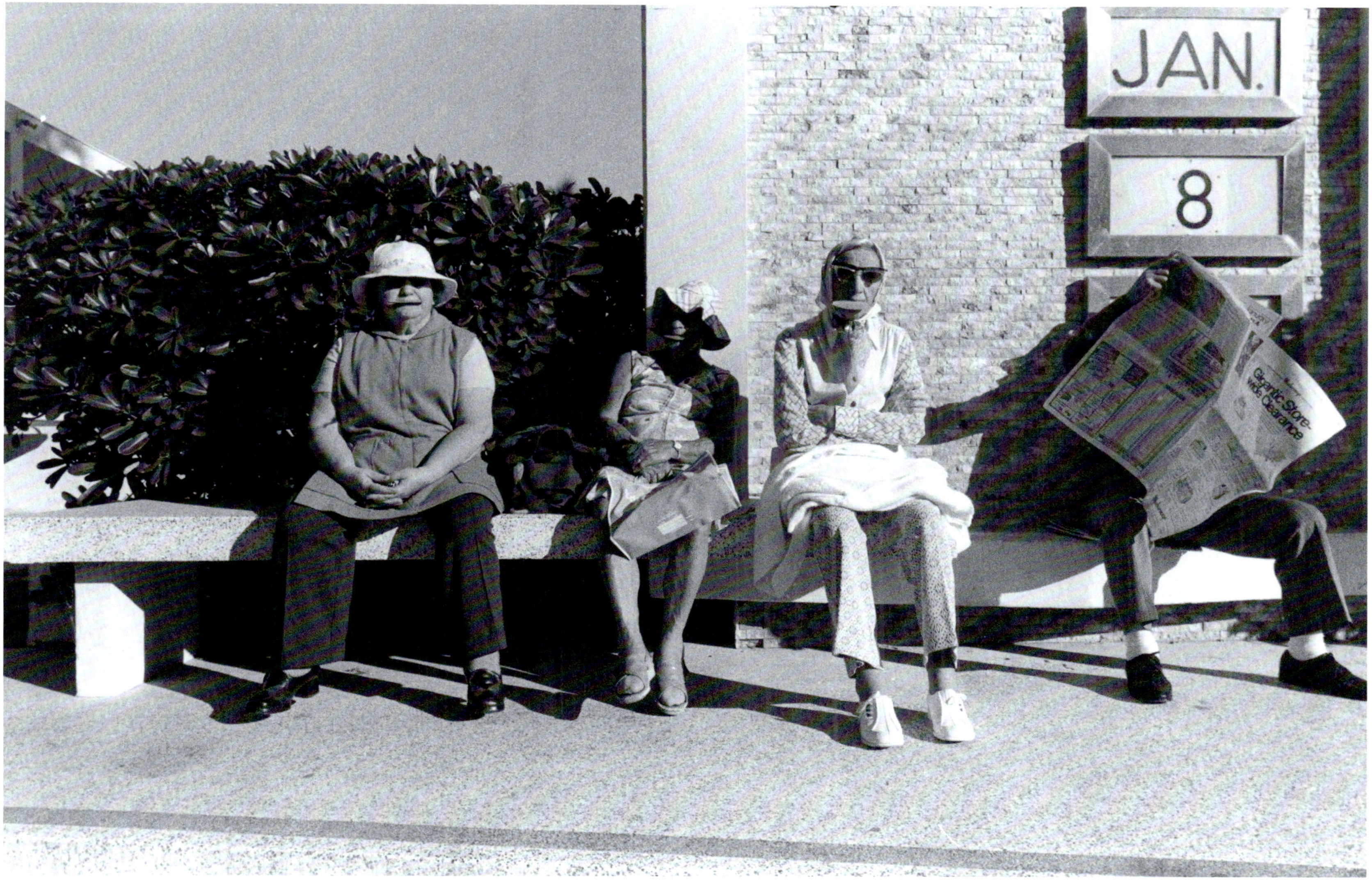
JAN.
8
Gigantic Store-wide Clearance

Women by Tenth Street Auditorium, 1981

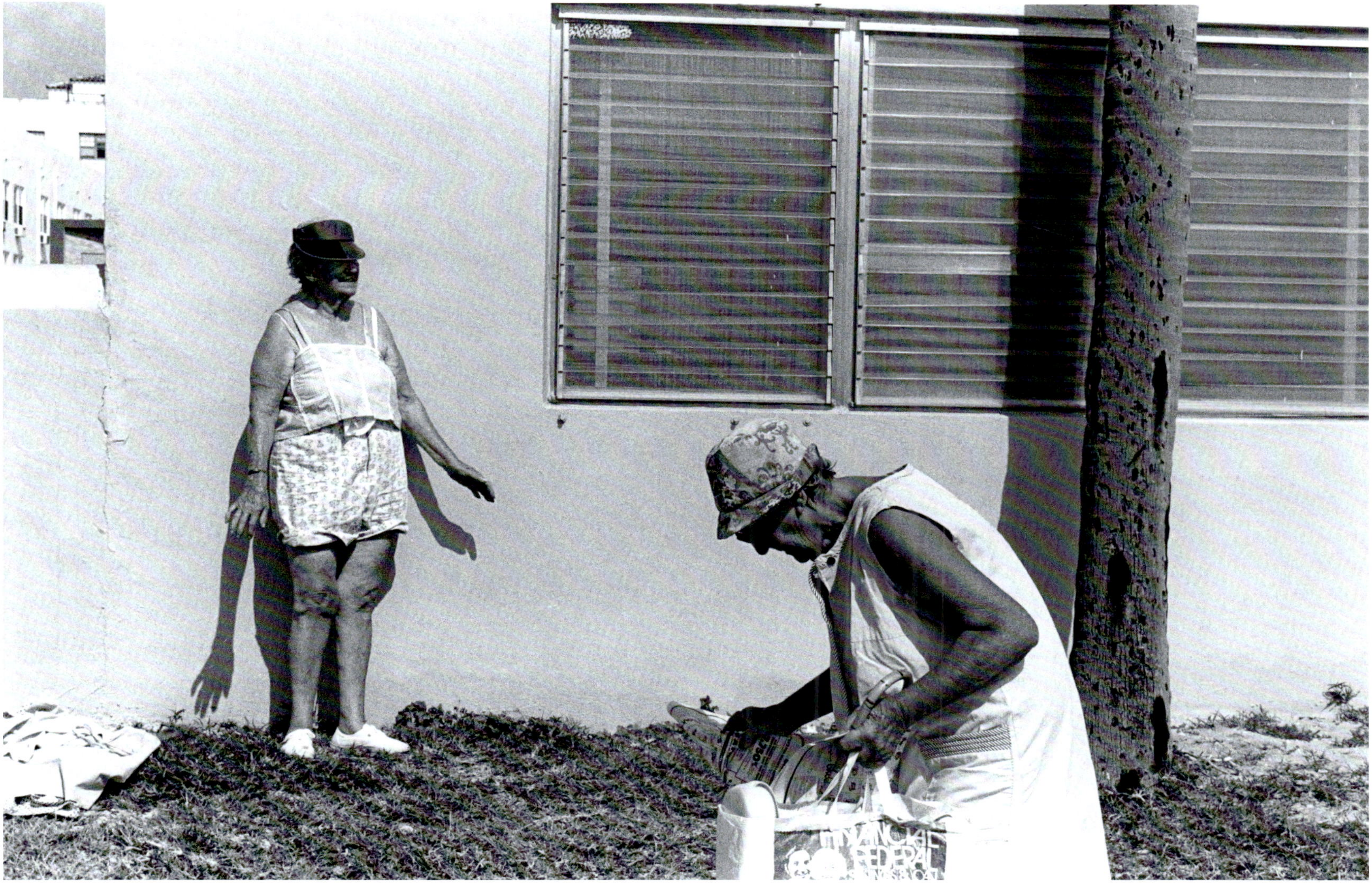
FEDERAL

Coral rock wall, 1977

The coral rock wall runs the length of Lummus Park, between Fifth Street and Fifteenth Street, and is an identifying feature. It divides the palm-covered grassy space and the beach, while enhancing the walk as it gracefully sweeps along the way.

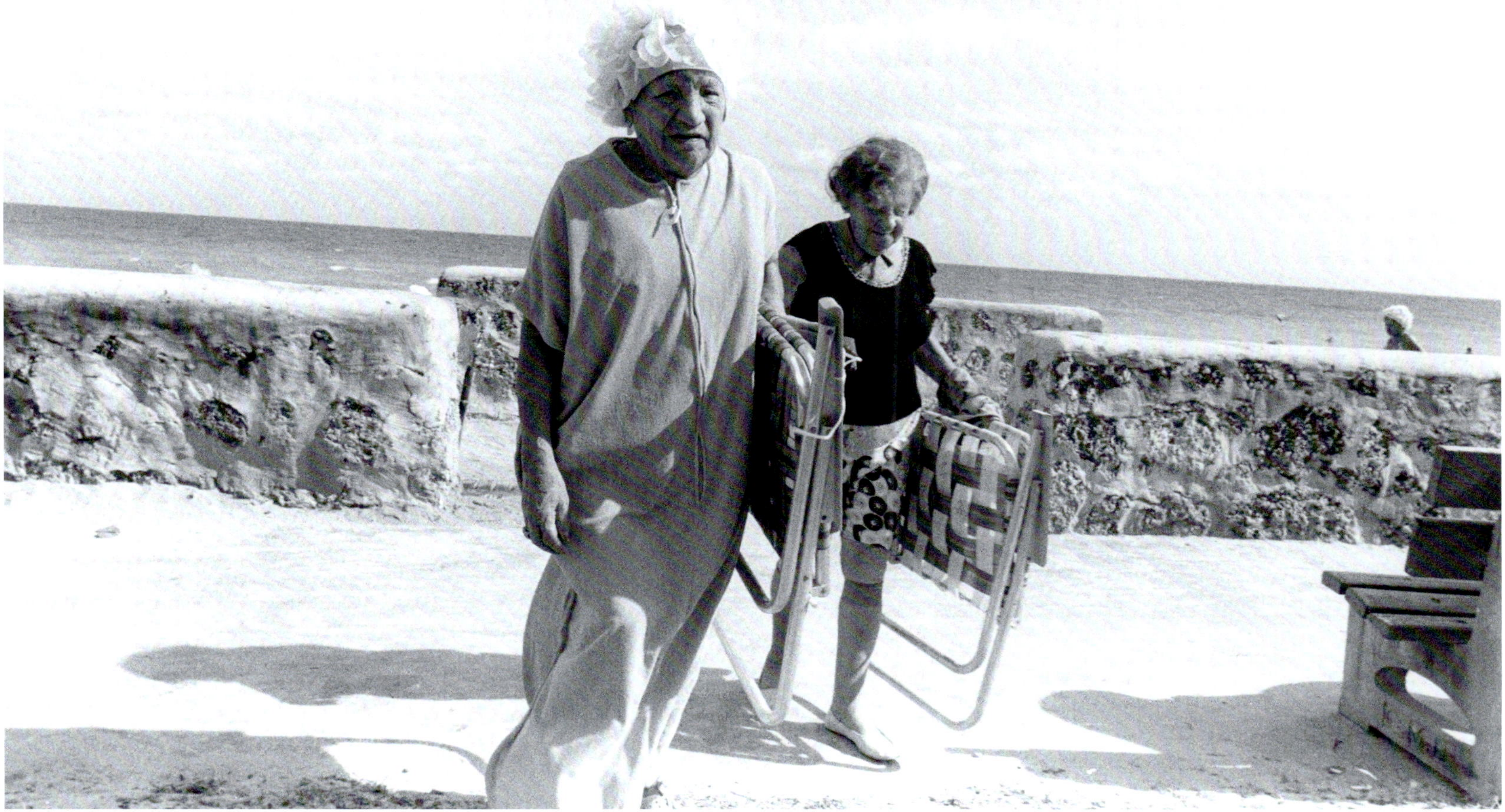

Women in ocean, 1981

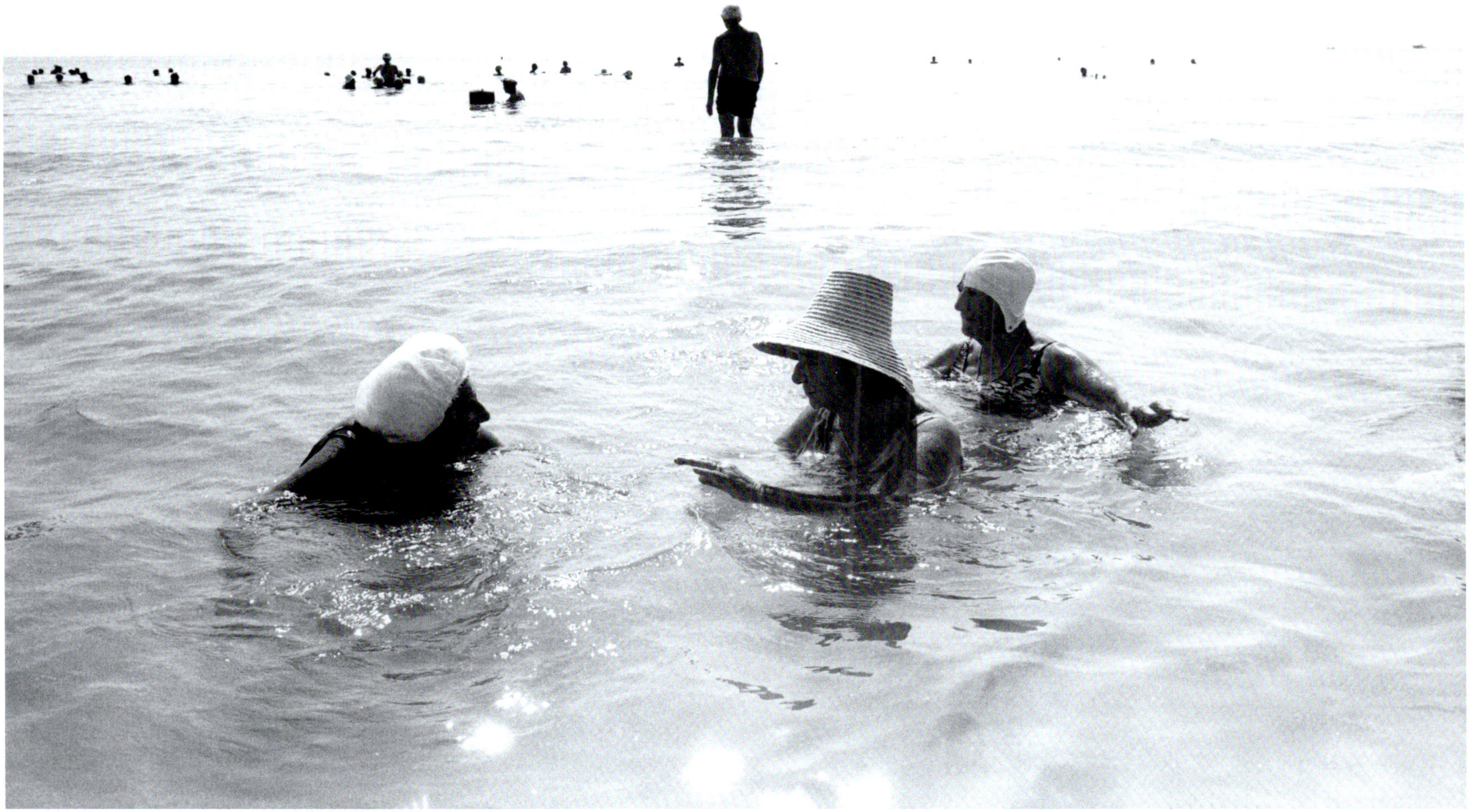

Bathing rope, 1986

Ropes were set at each street along the beach as safety features.

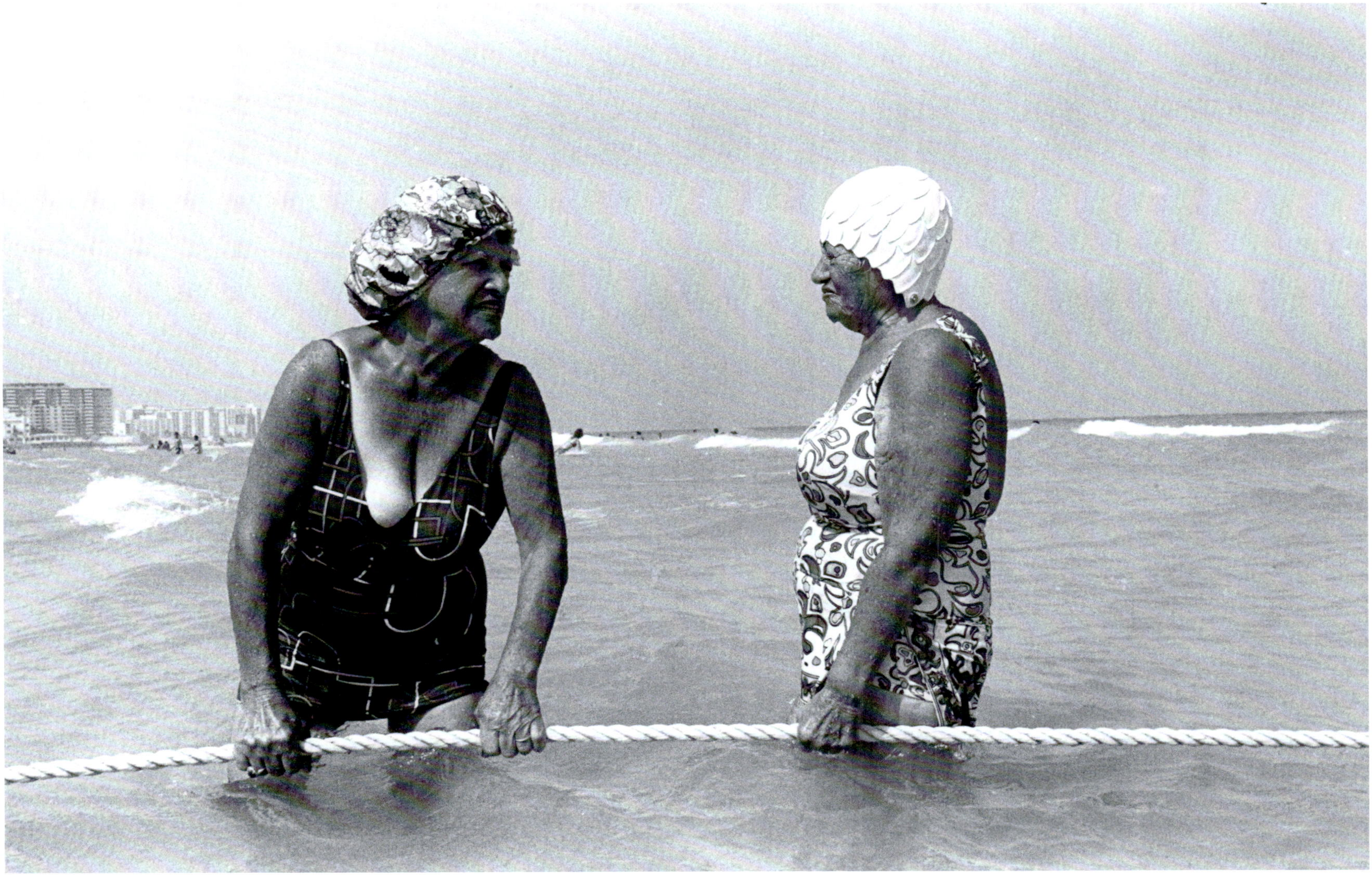

Man sitting on coral rock wall, 1977

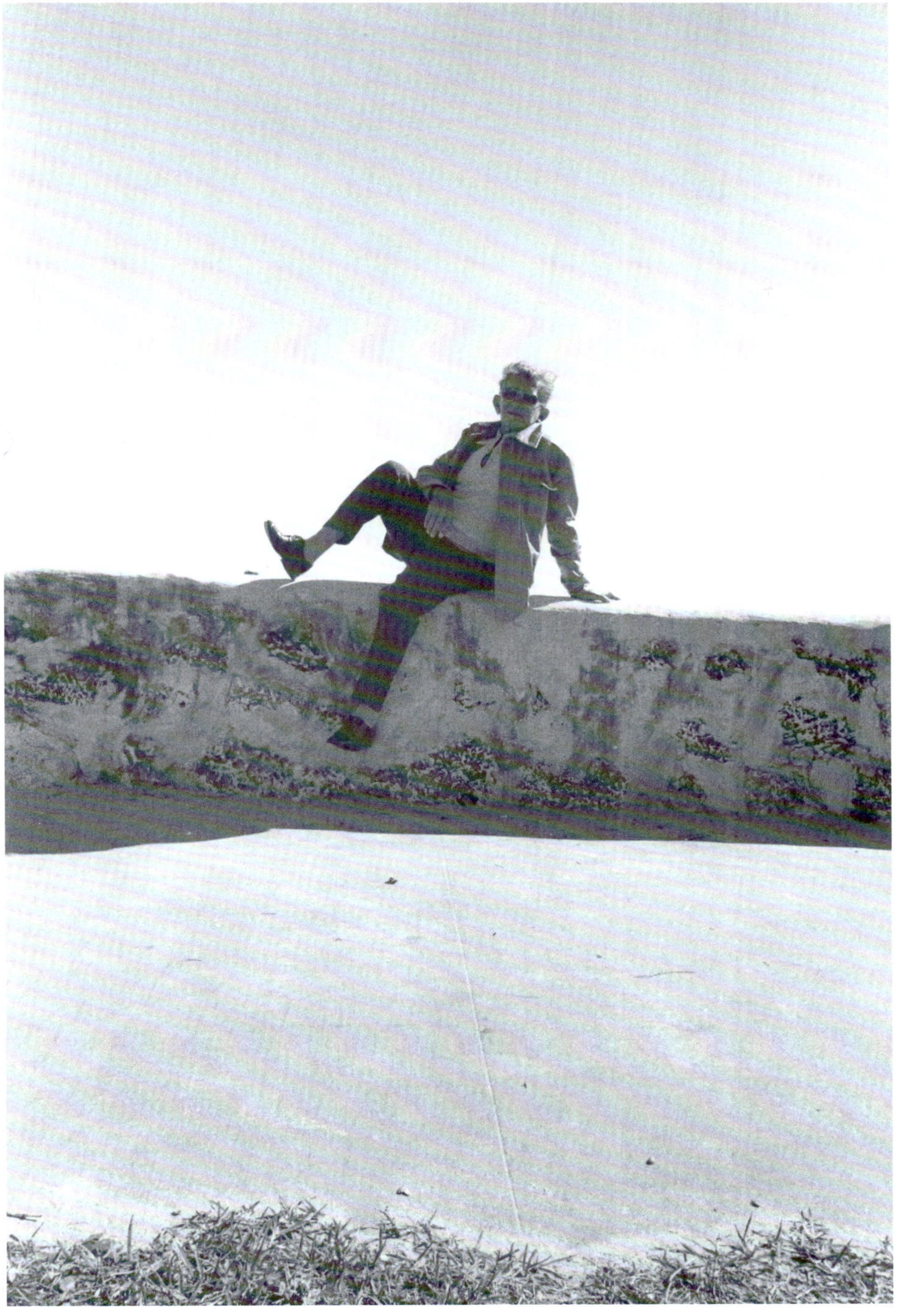

Woman at beach by coral rock wall, 1978

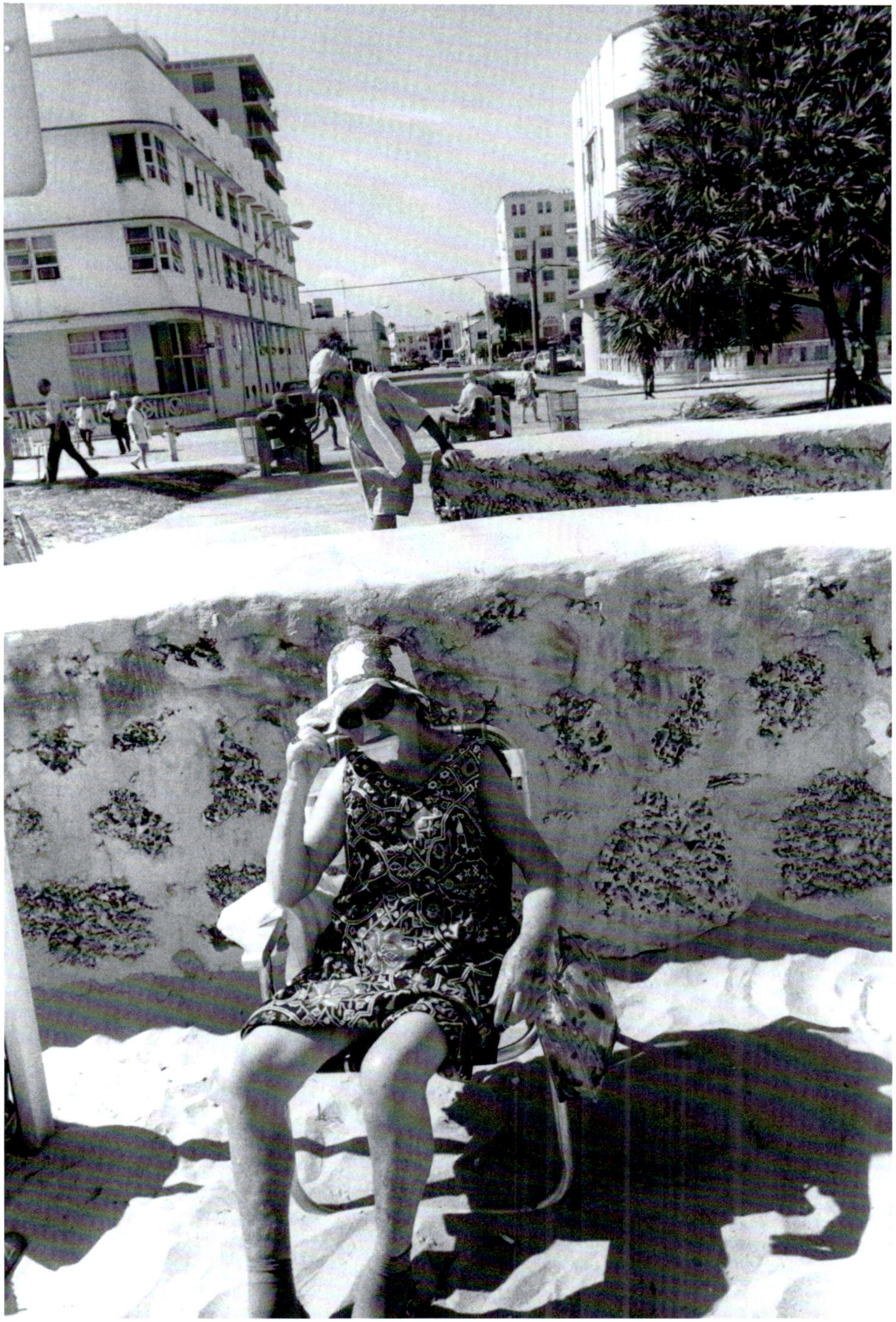

People talking by Ninth Street bandshell at Lummus Park, 1984

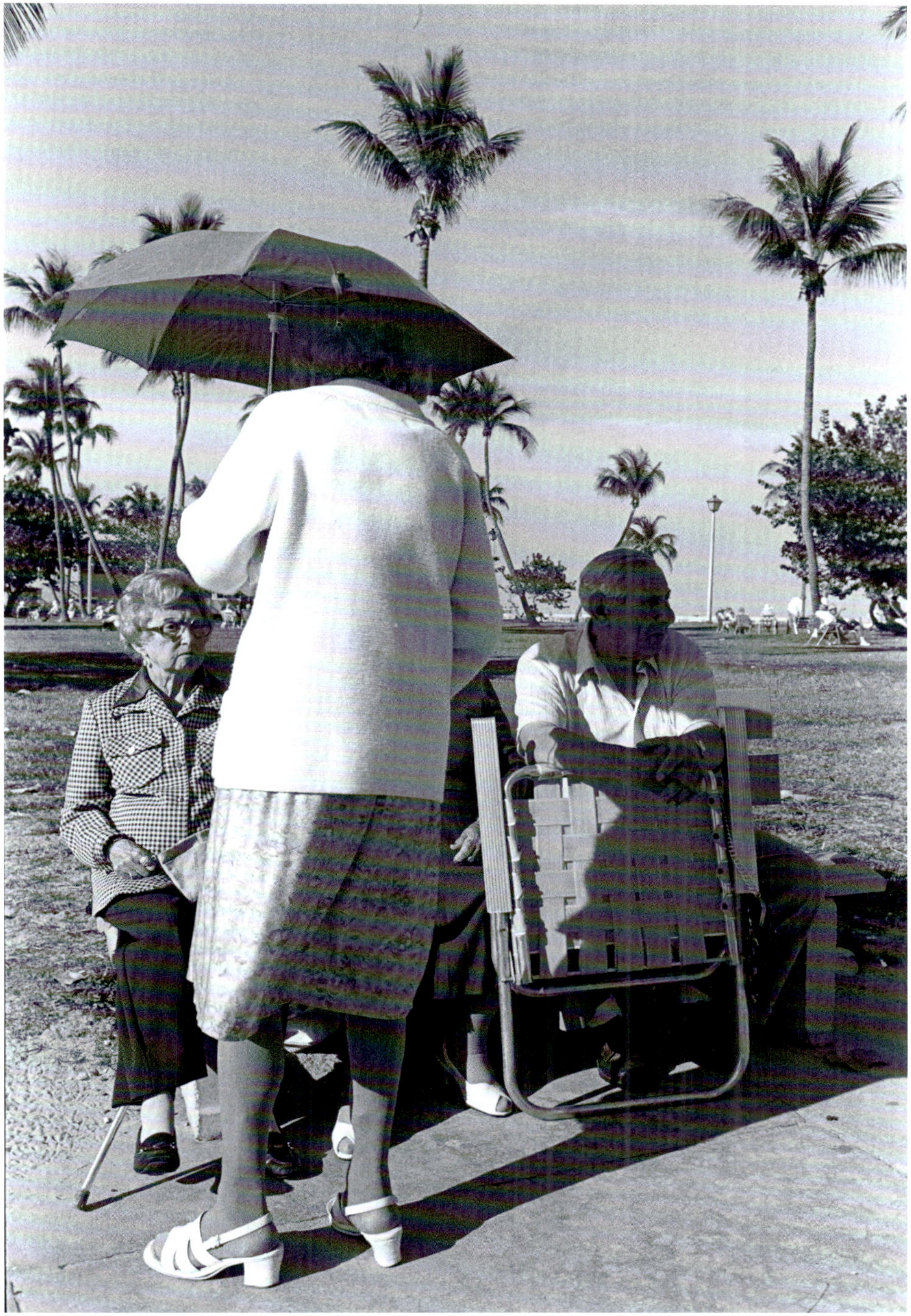

Lummus Park, 1977

Lummus Park was central to life in South Beach. People would bring their folding lawn chairs here to enjoy an afternoon of socializing.

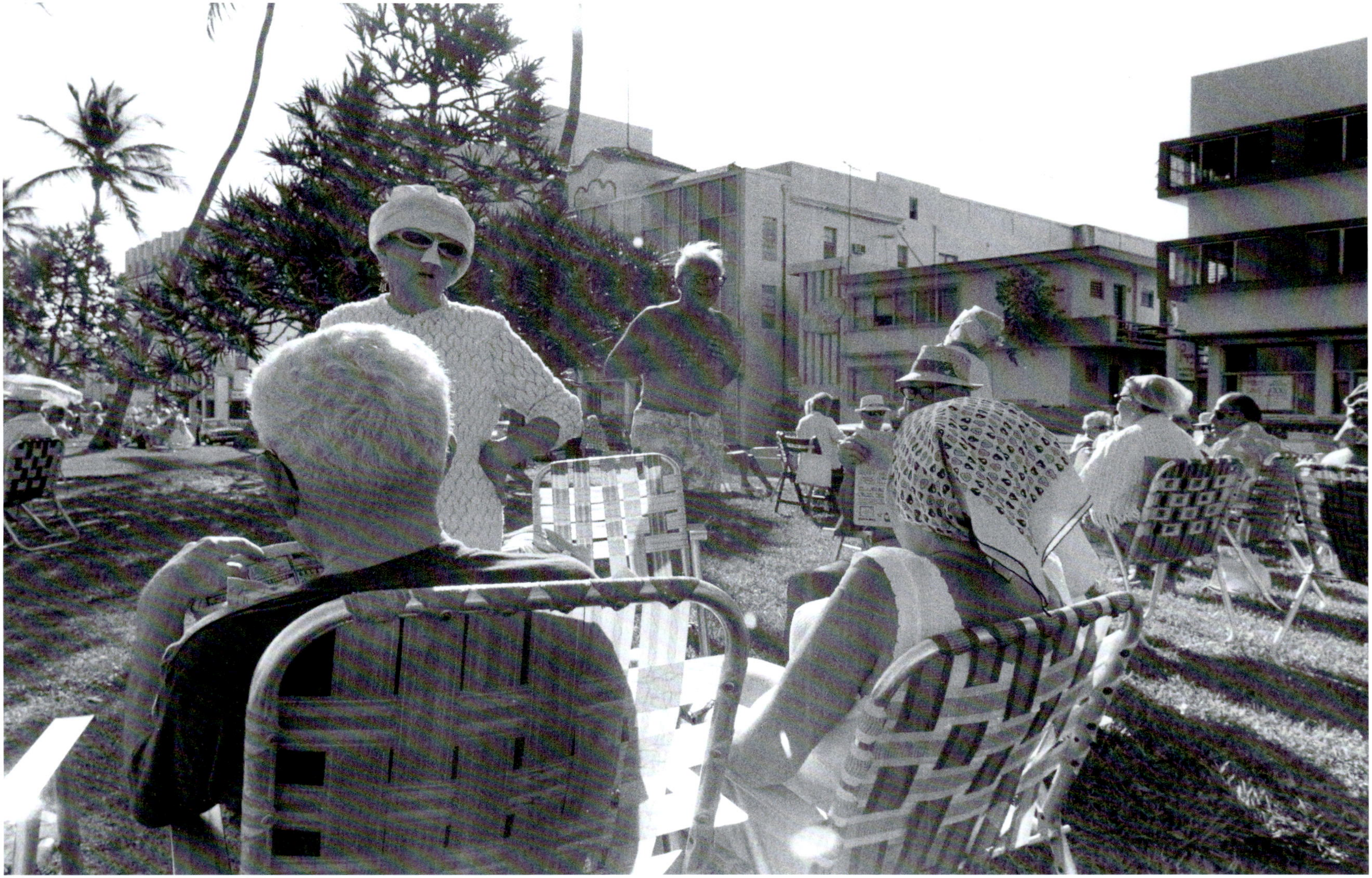

Women talking, 1984

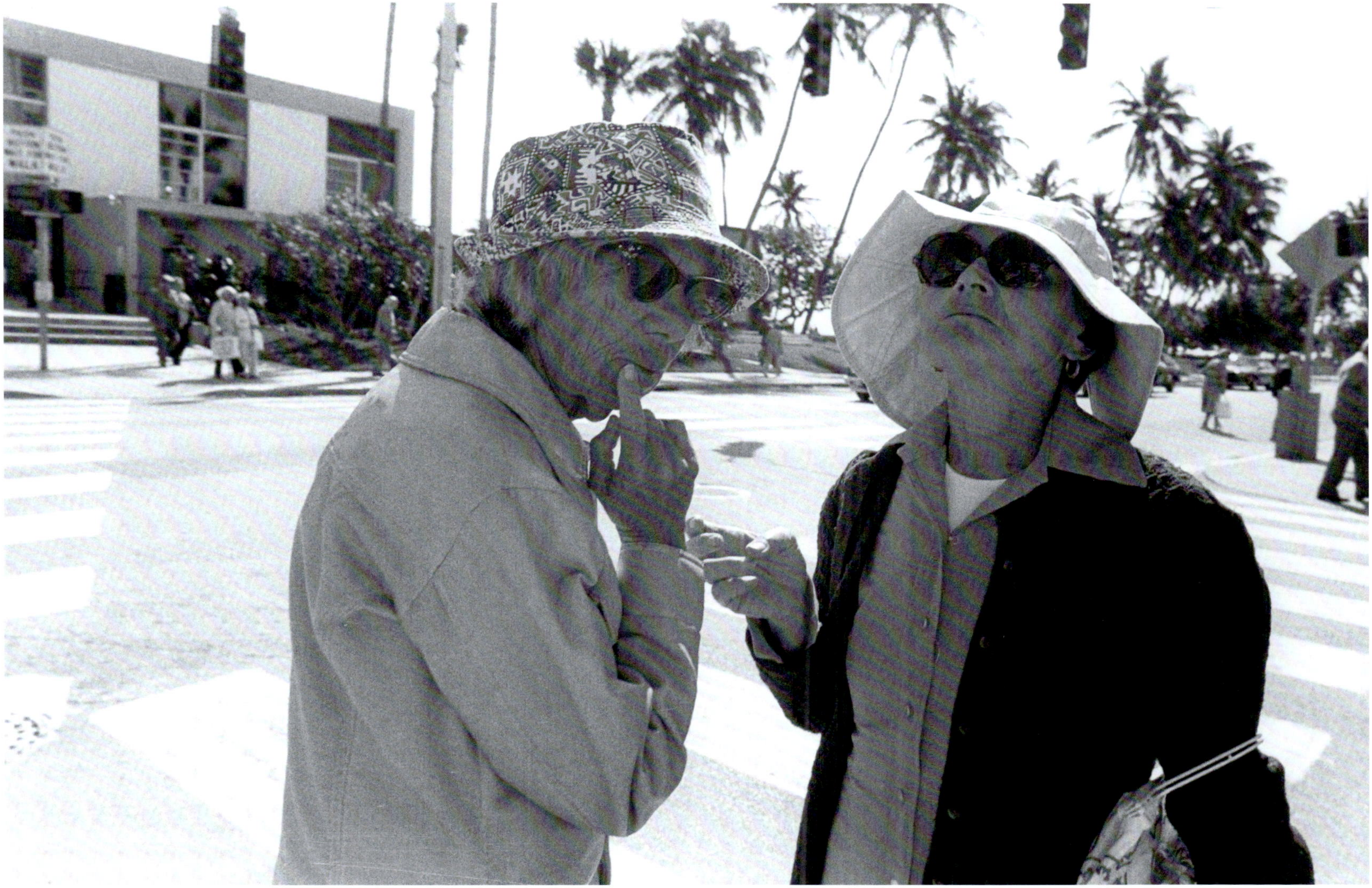

Women poolside, 1977

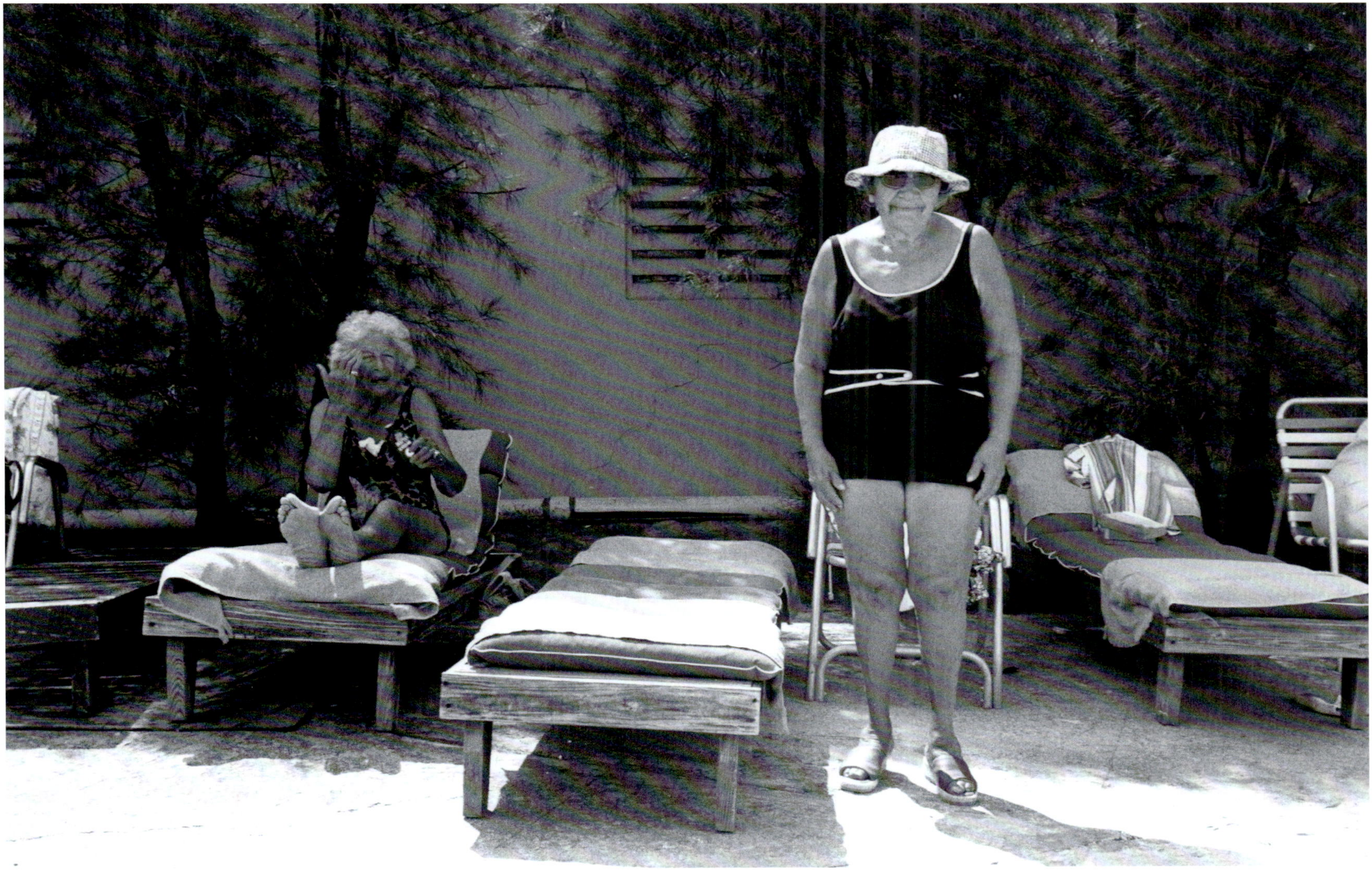

Couple by cabana, 1977

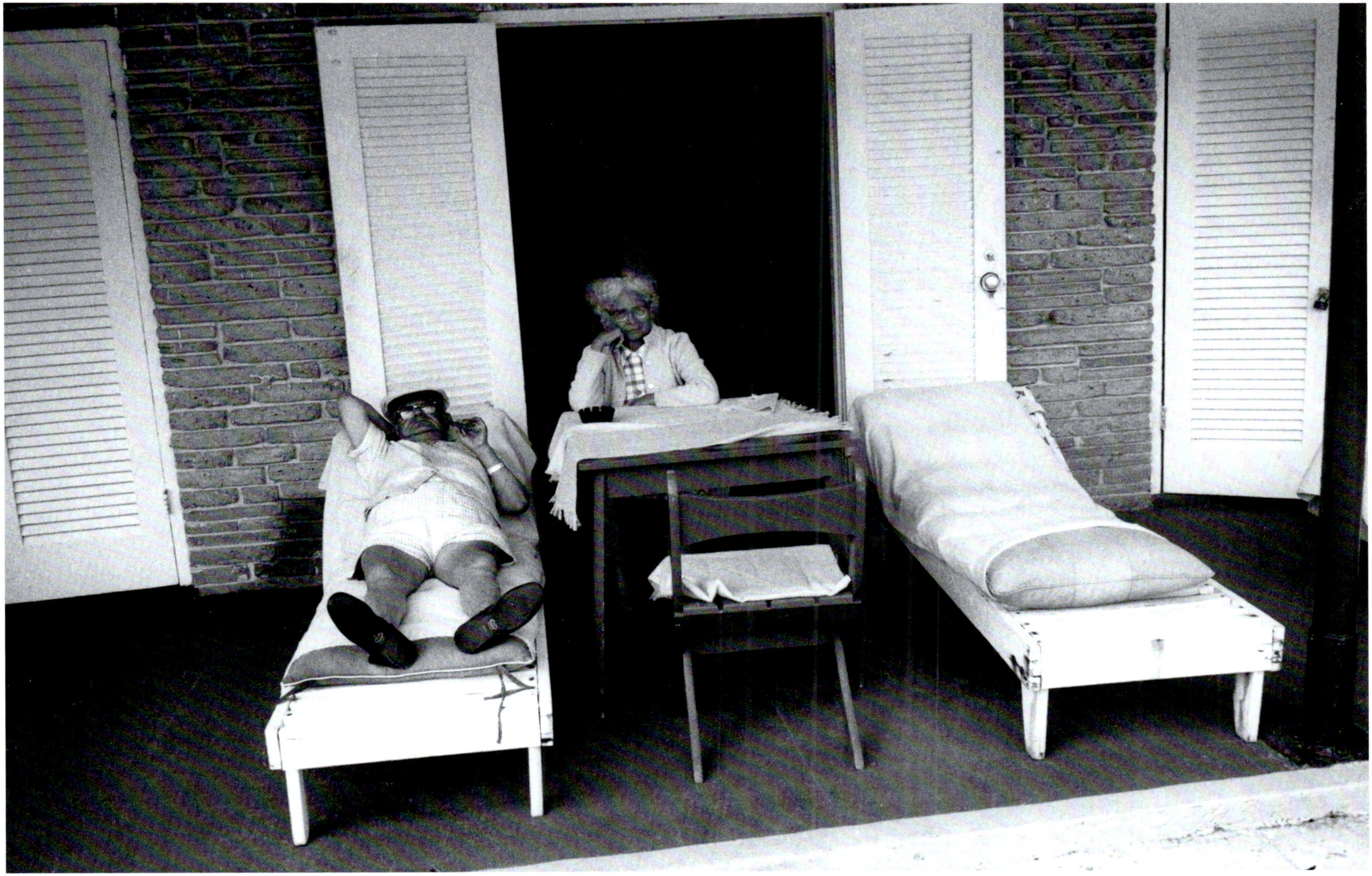

Woman with caregiver, 1984

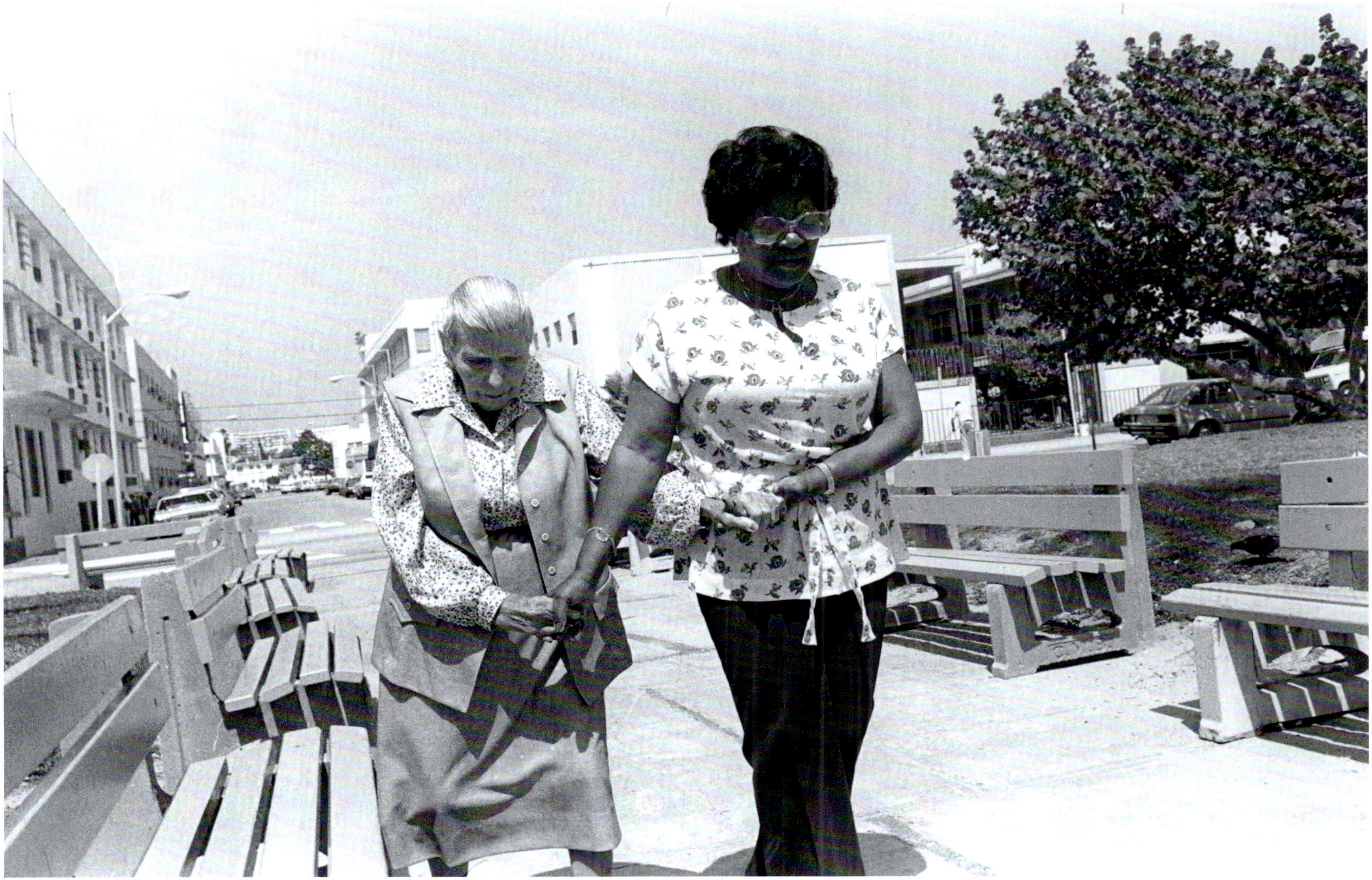

Women on hotel porch, 1981

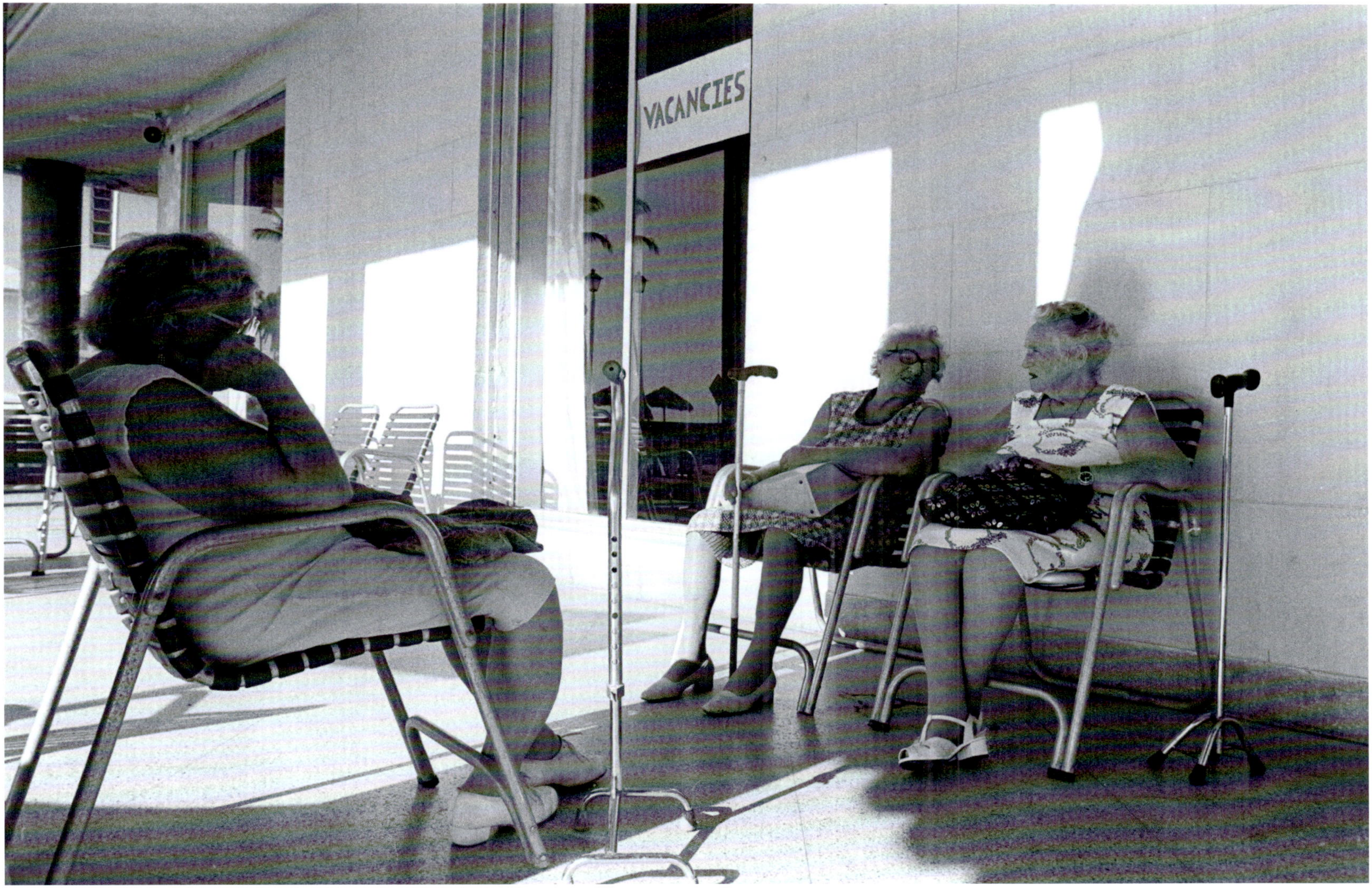
VACANCIES

Woman by hotel, 1979

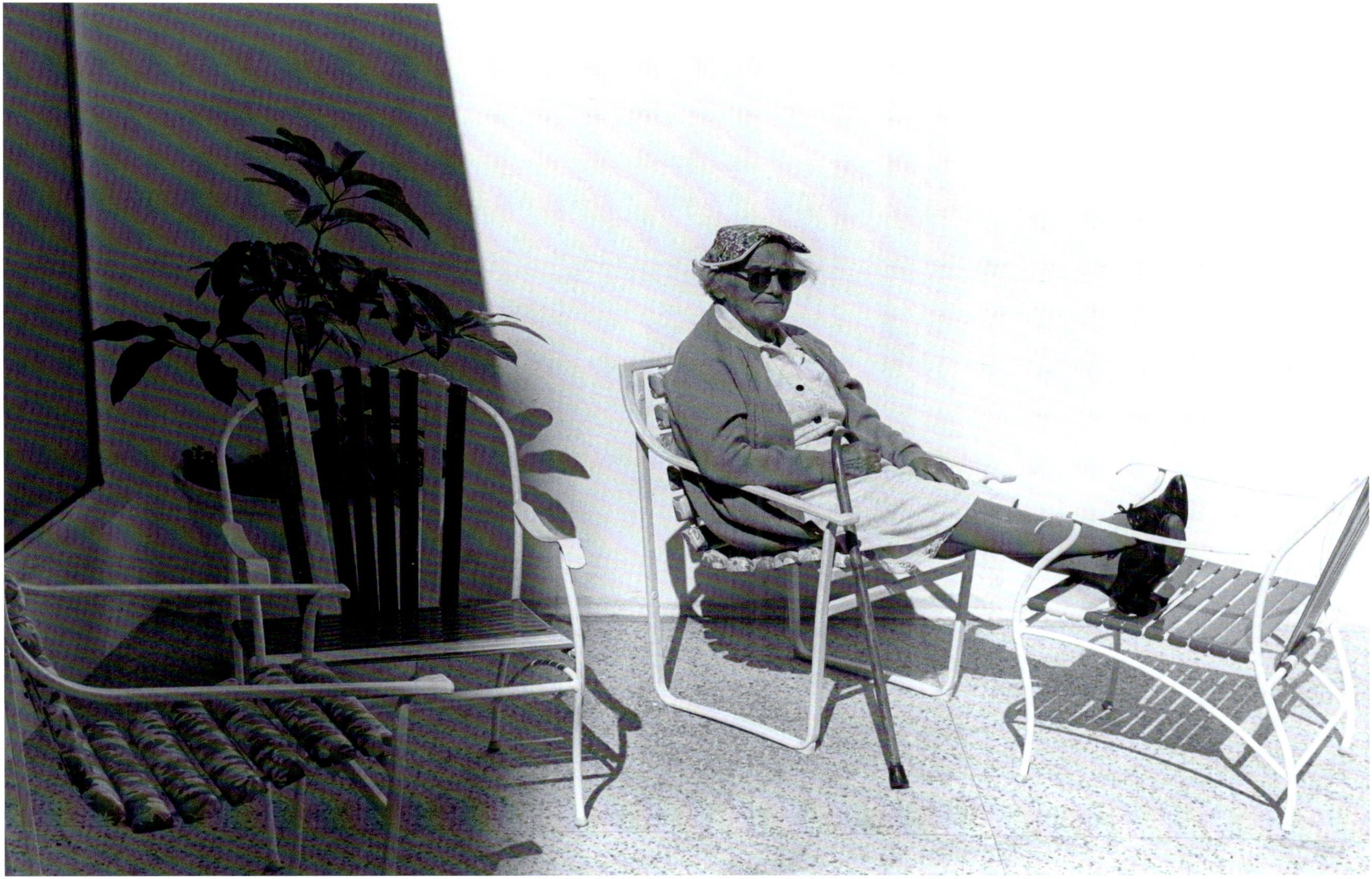

People walking along Sixth Street, 1978

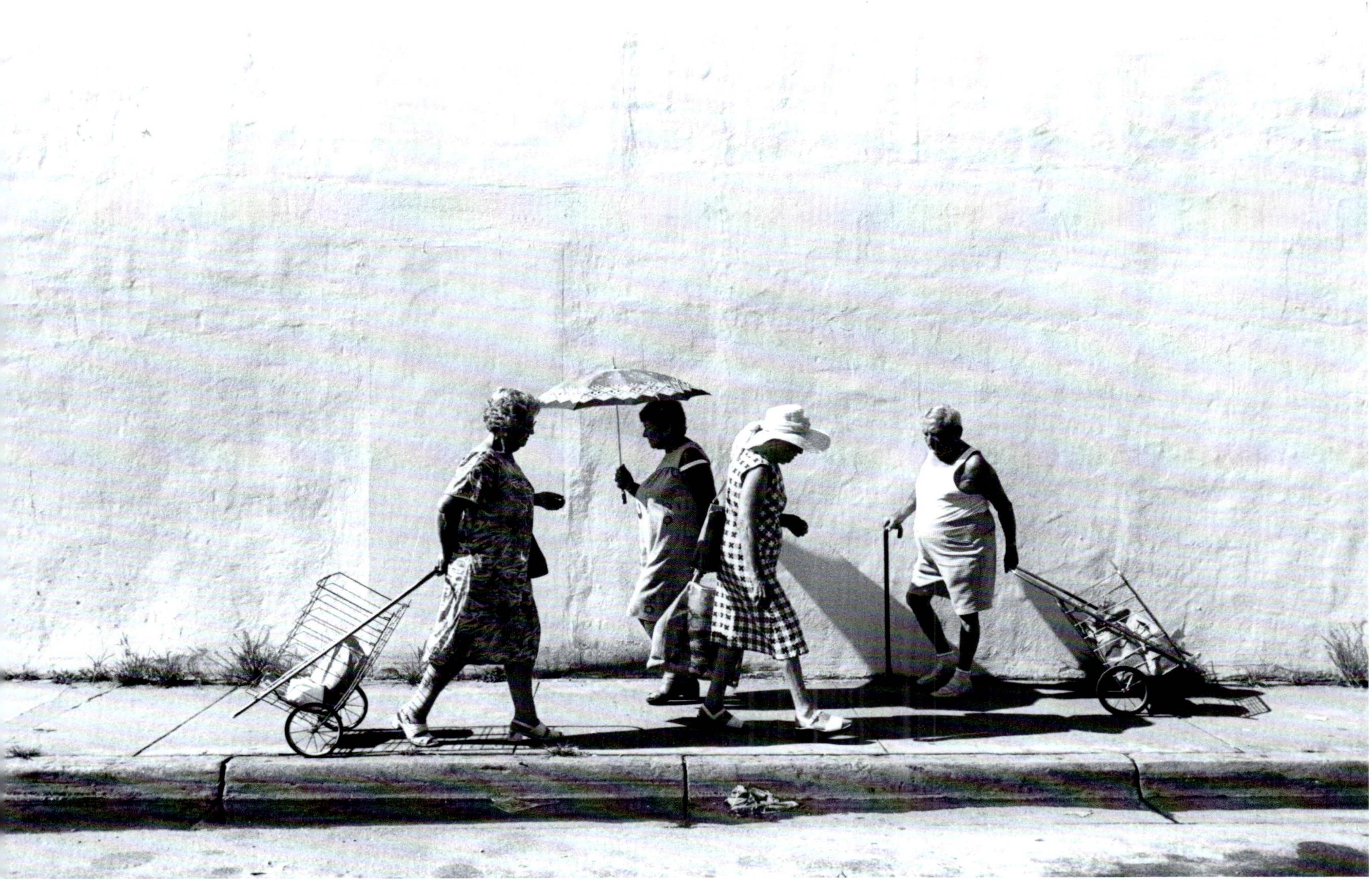

Senior citizens' orchestra, 1977

The senior citizens' orchestra practiced at Sixth Street Community Center.

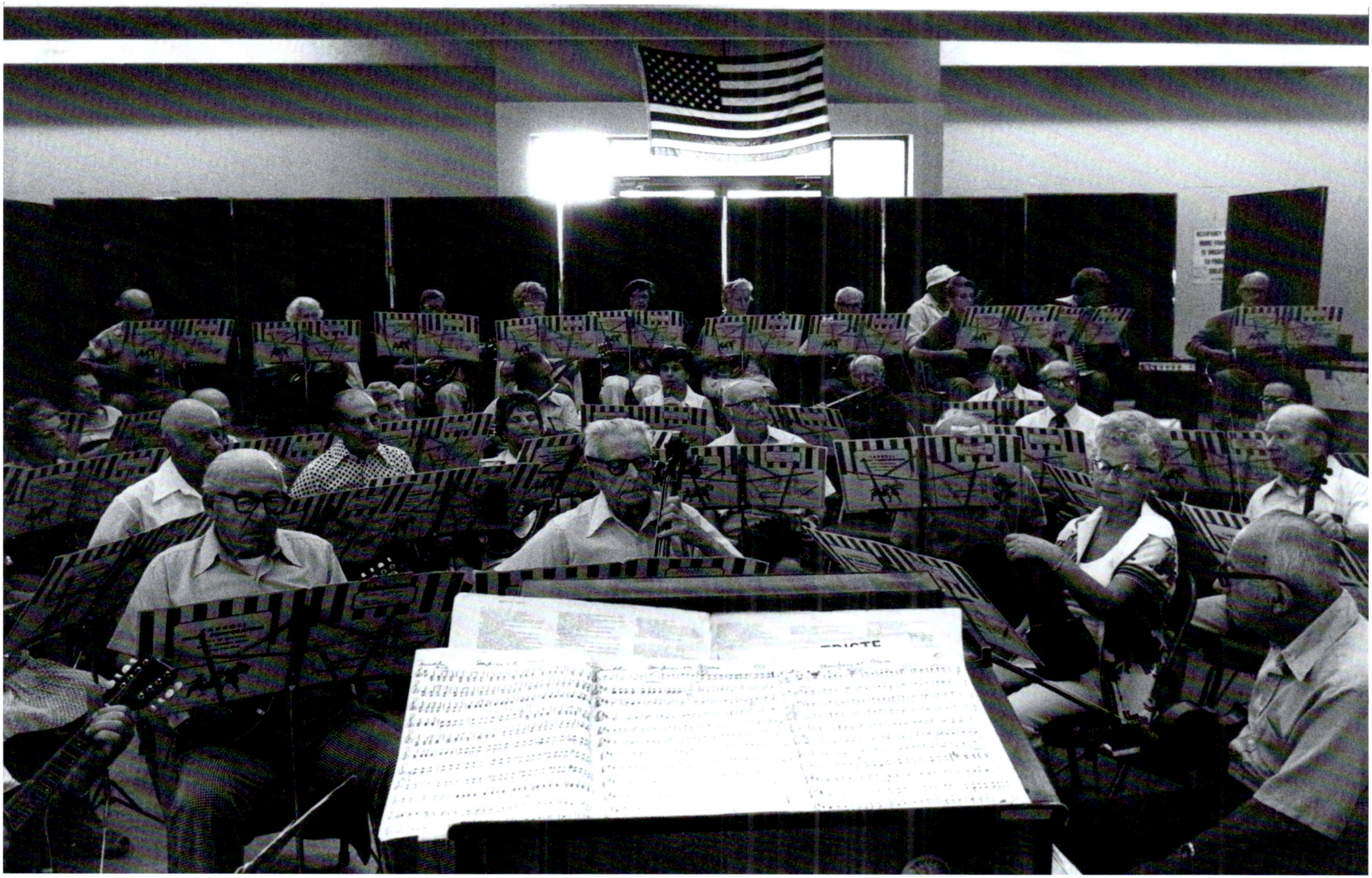

Exercising in bank, 1986

Activities were plentiful, such as exercise classes in a room located in a bank building.

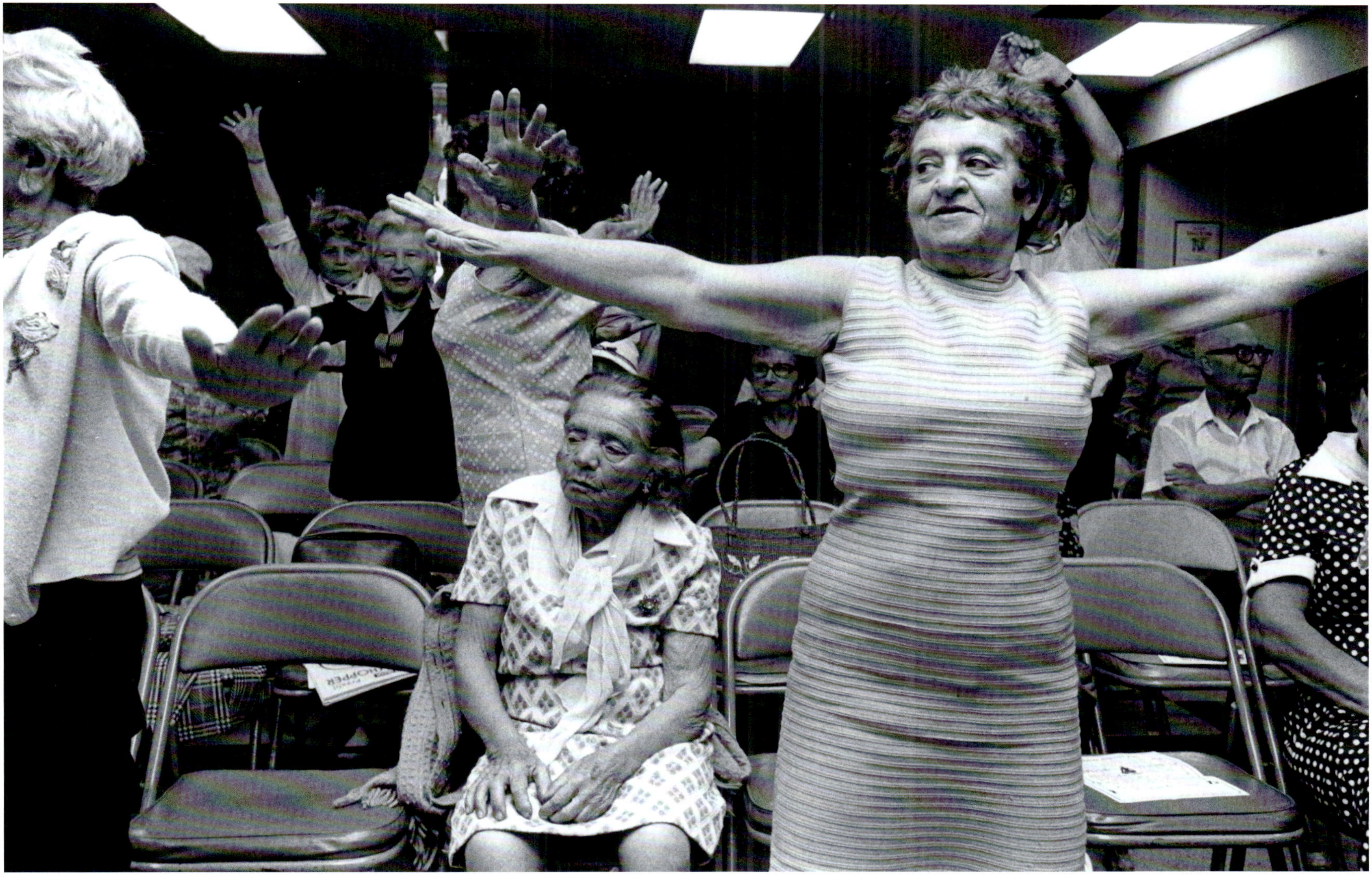

Guild for the Blind, 1977

The Miami Beach Guild for the Blind met at the Twenty-First Street Community Center.

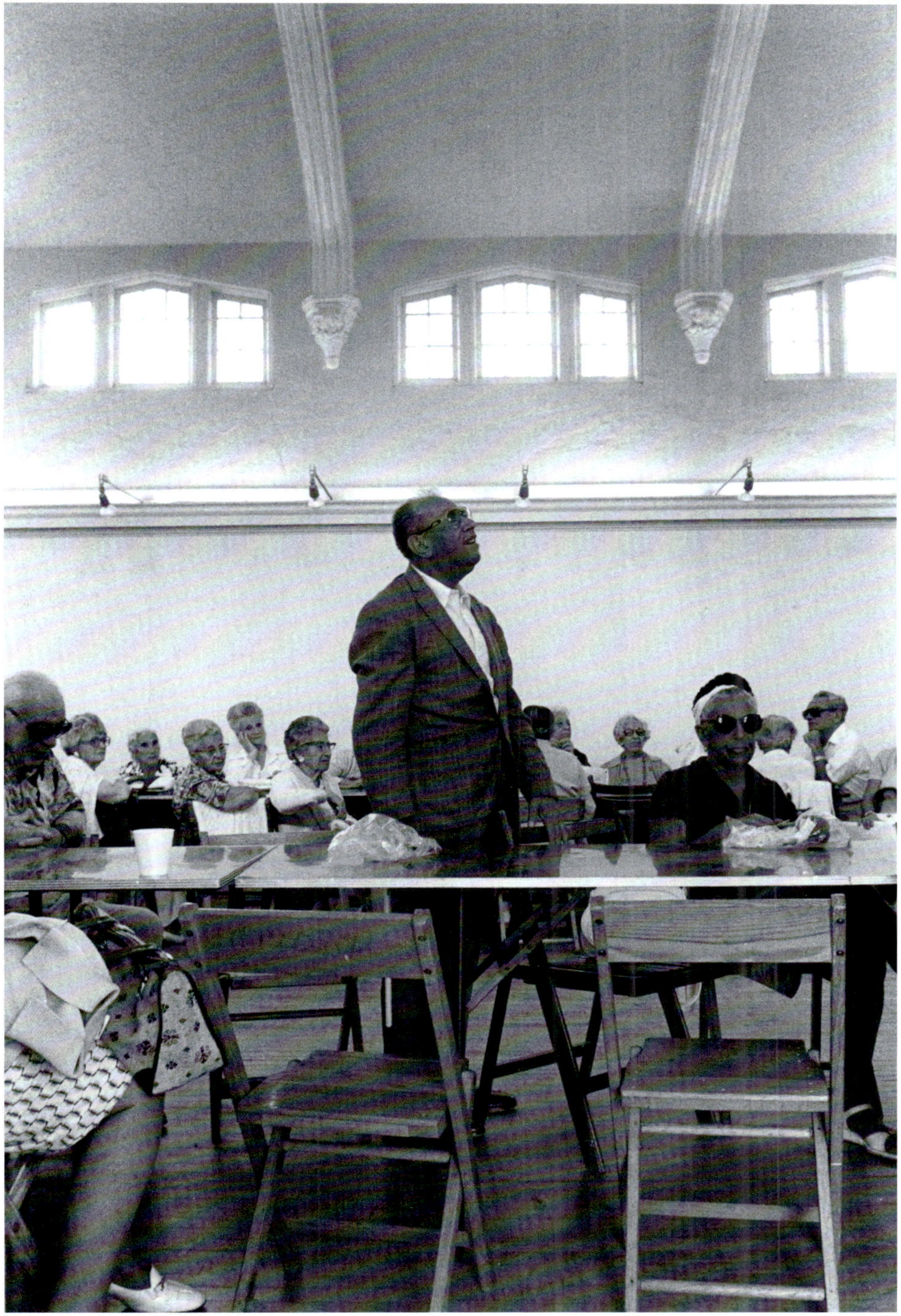

Shoppers at Washington Avenue, 1981

Washington Avenue was the central place for grocery stores, beauty parlors, and bakeries. Everything was within walking distance, forming a self-contained community.

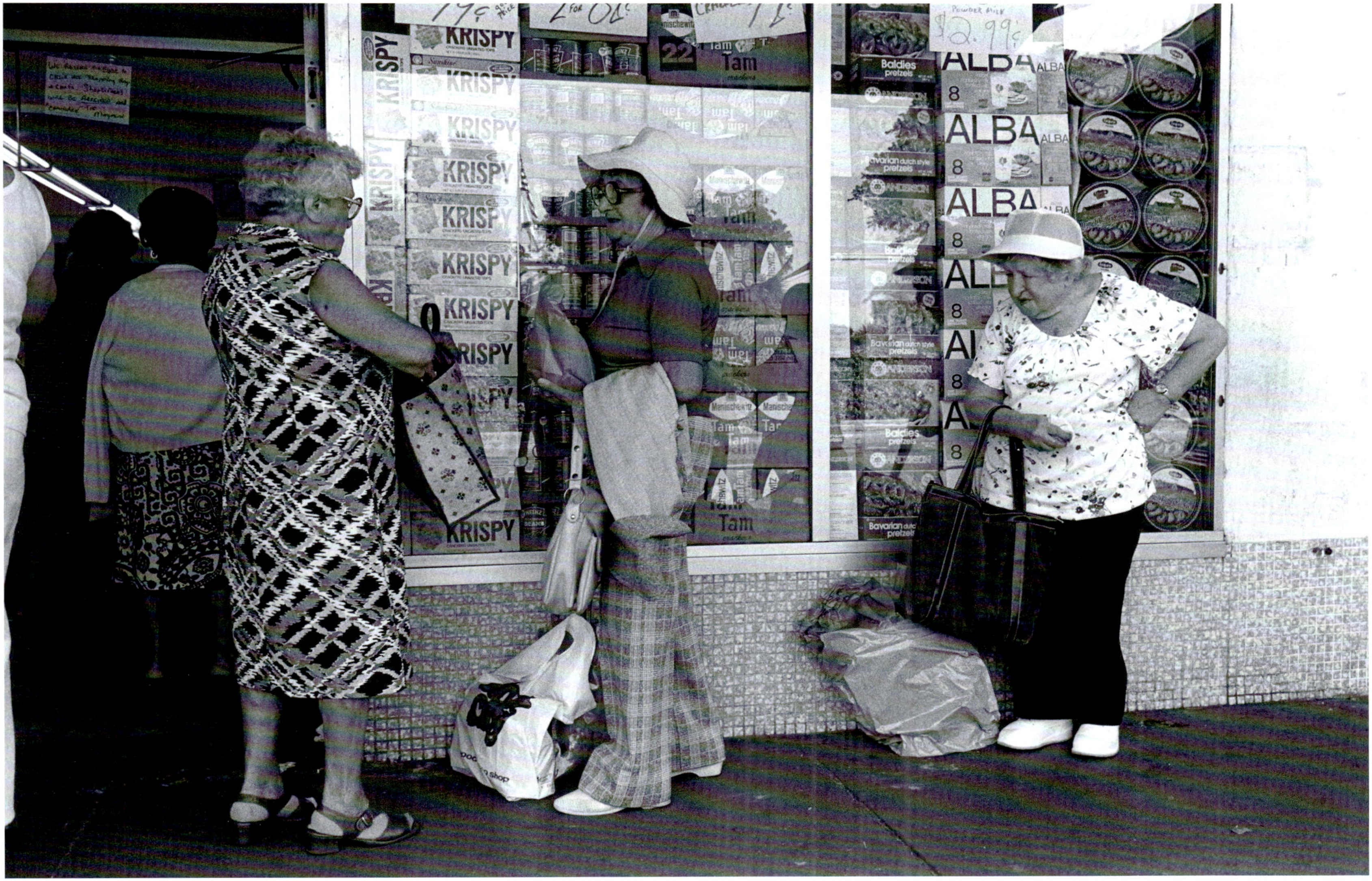
KRISPY
Tam Tam
Manischewitz
Baldies pretzels
Bavarian dutch style pretzels
ALBA
Powder Milk
$2.99¢

Lobby of the Kenmore Hotel, 1980

Hotels situated on corner lots, like the Kenmore, were designed more finely than most others.

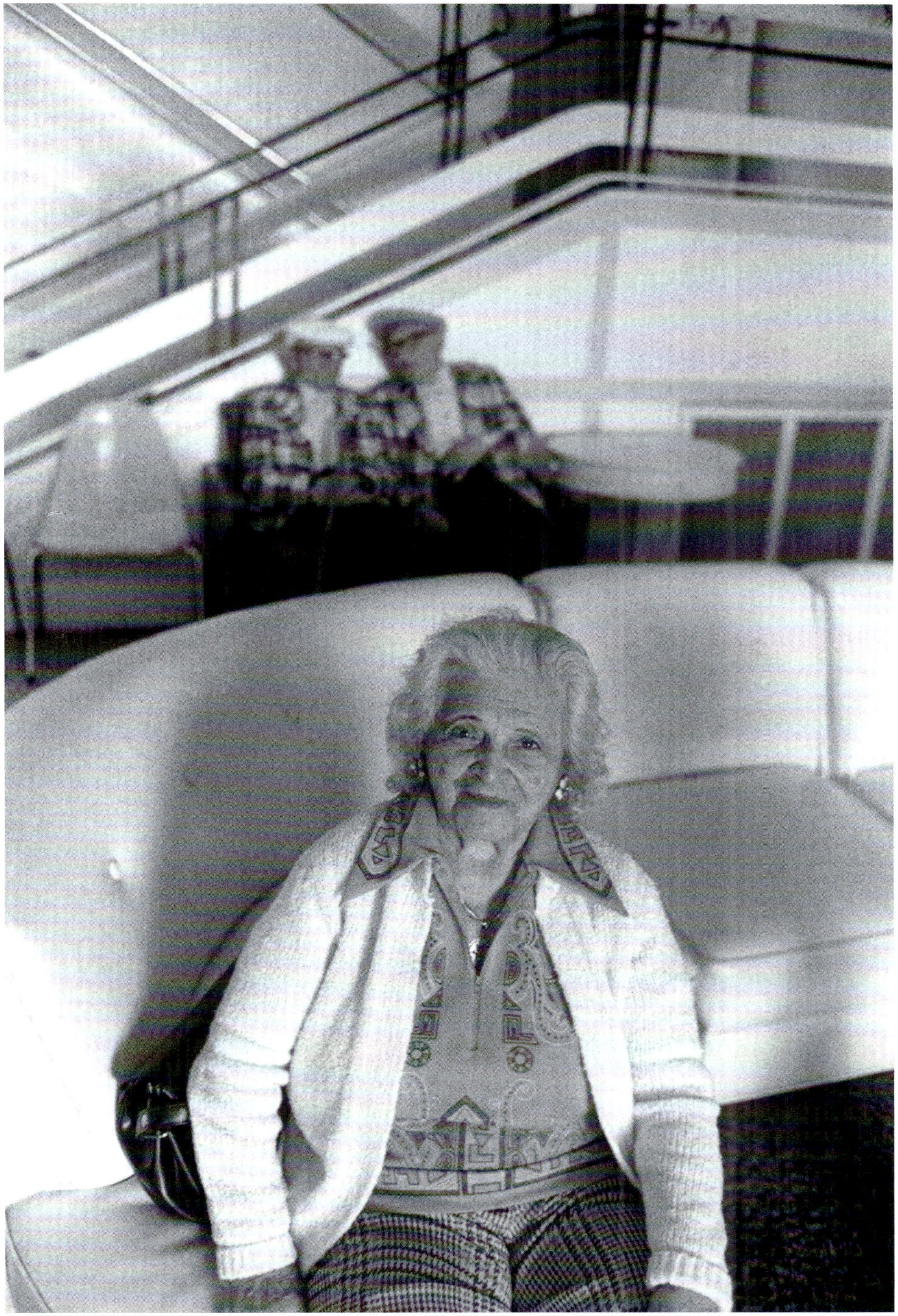

Man mounting stairs of Alamac Hotel, 1983

One of the grander hotels along Collins Avenue, a block west of Ocean Drive, the Alamac Hotel, like others, was seasonal. The Alamac boasted of having a saltwater swimming pool.

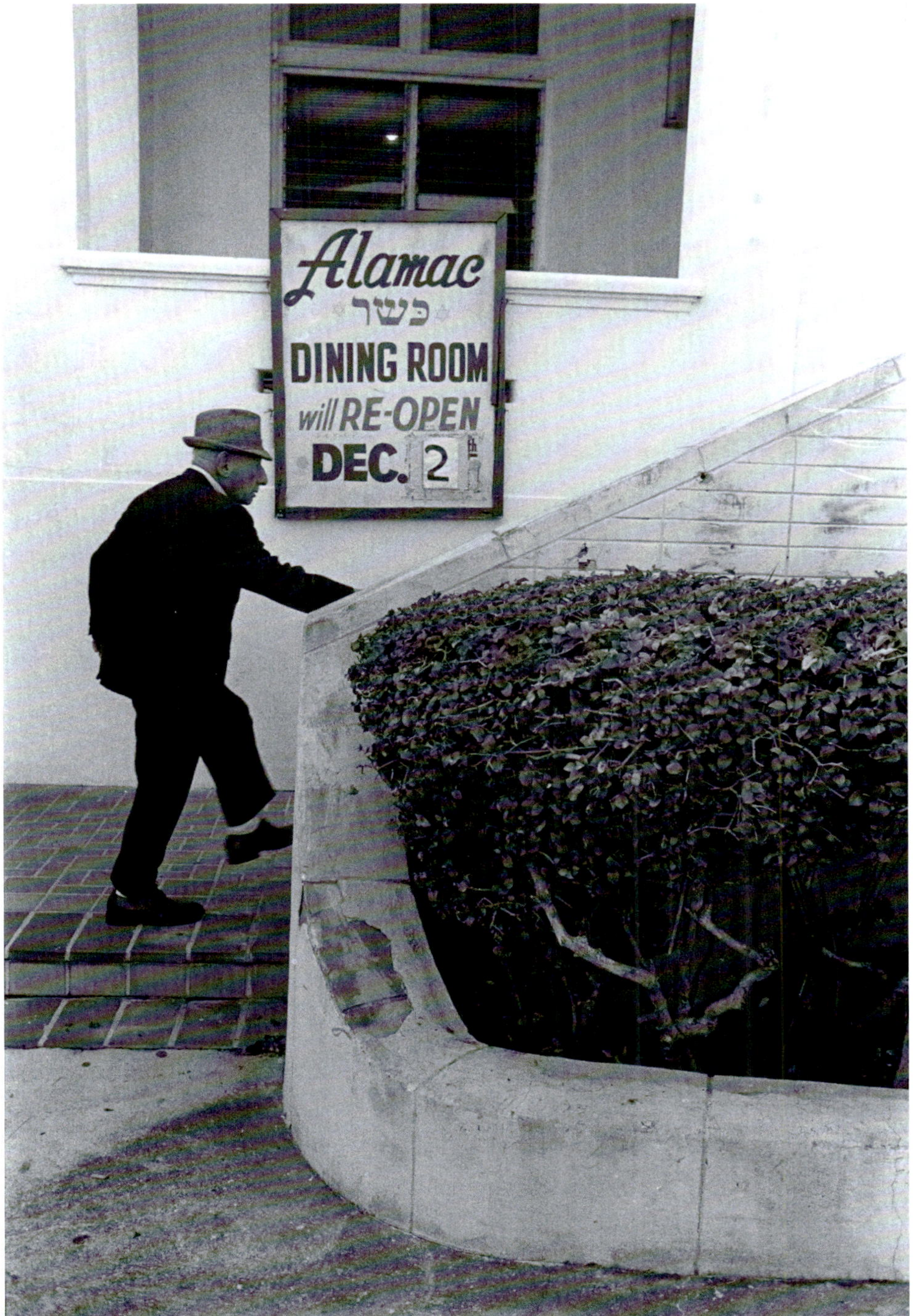
Alamac
כשר
DINING ROOM
will RE-OPEN
DEC. 2

People at apartment building, 1978

Modest apartment buildings, generally two or three stories, filled the interior of South Beach, from Washington Avenue west to Biscayne Bay.

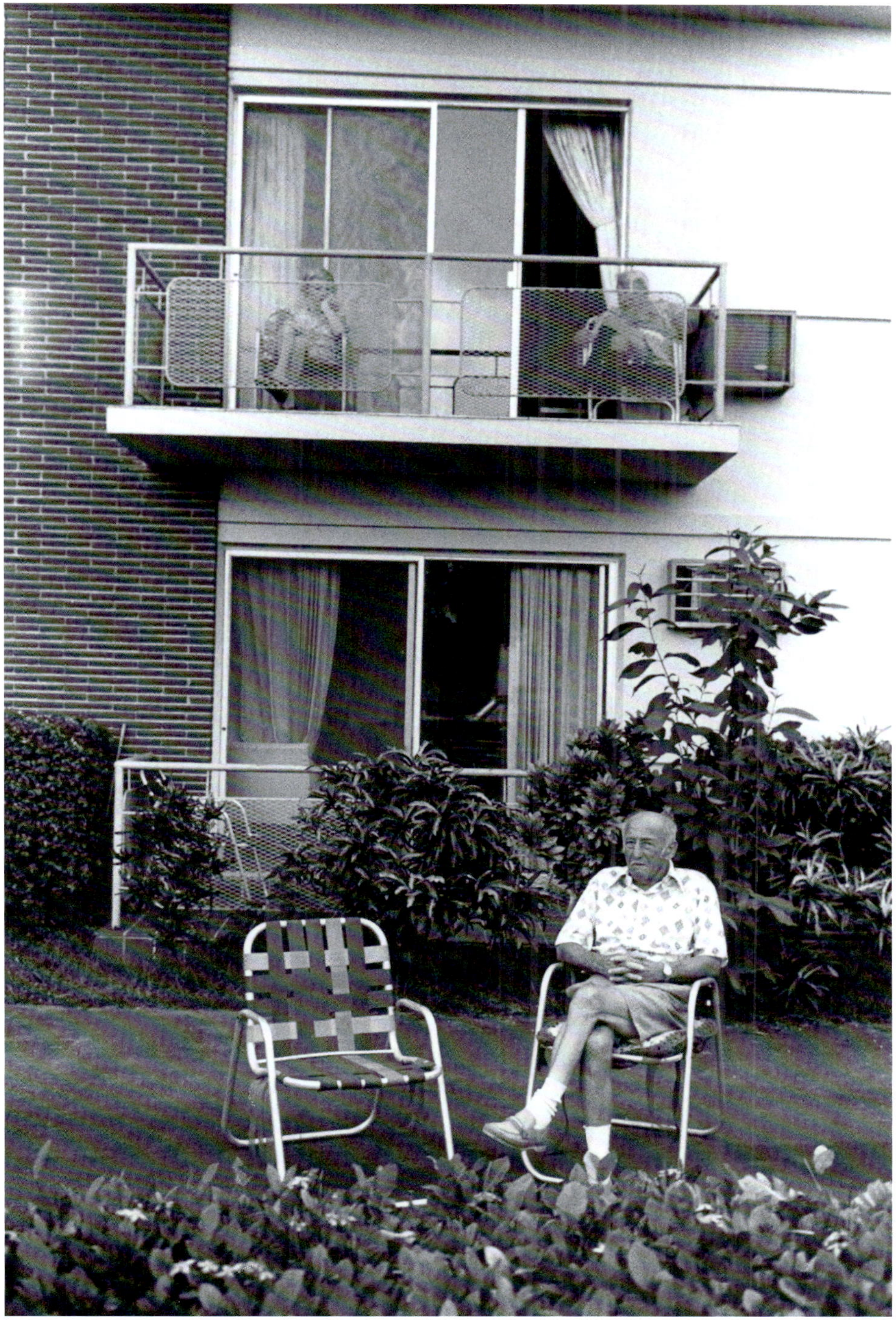

Street scene, 1983

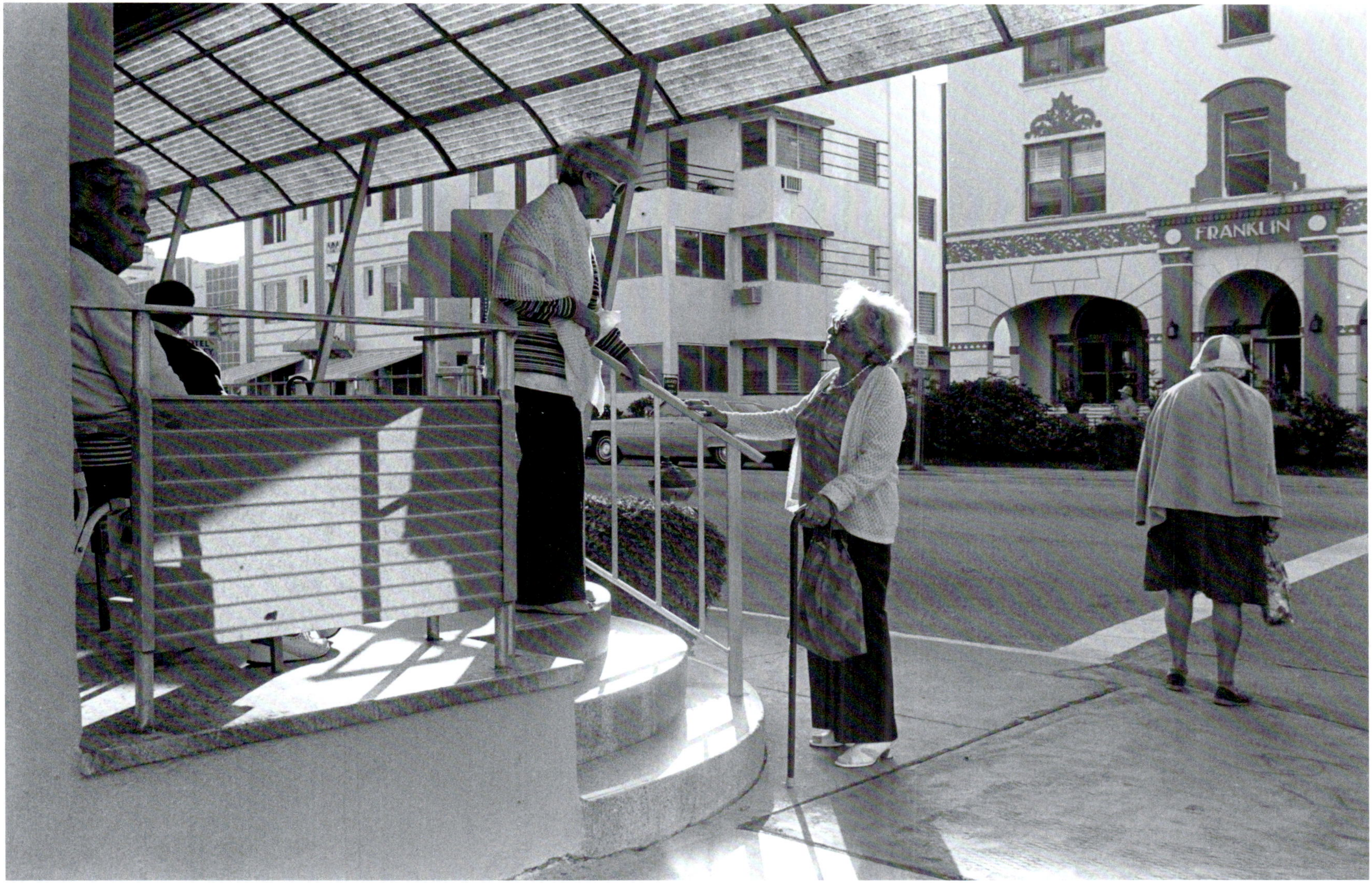
FRANKLIN

Couple and woman at Ninth Street bandshell, 1984

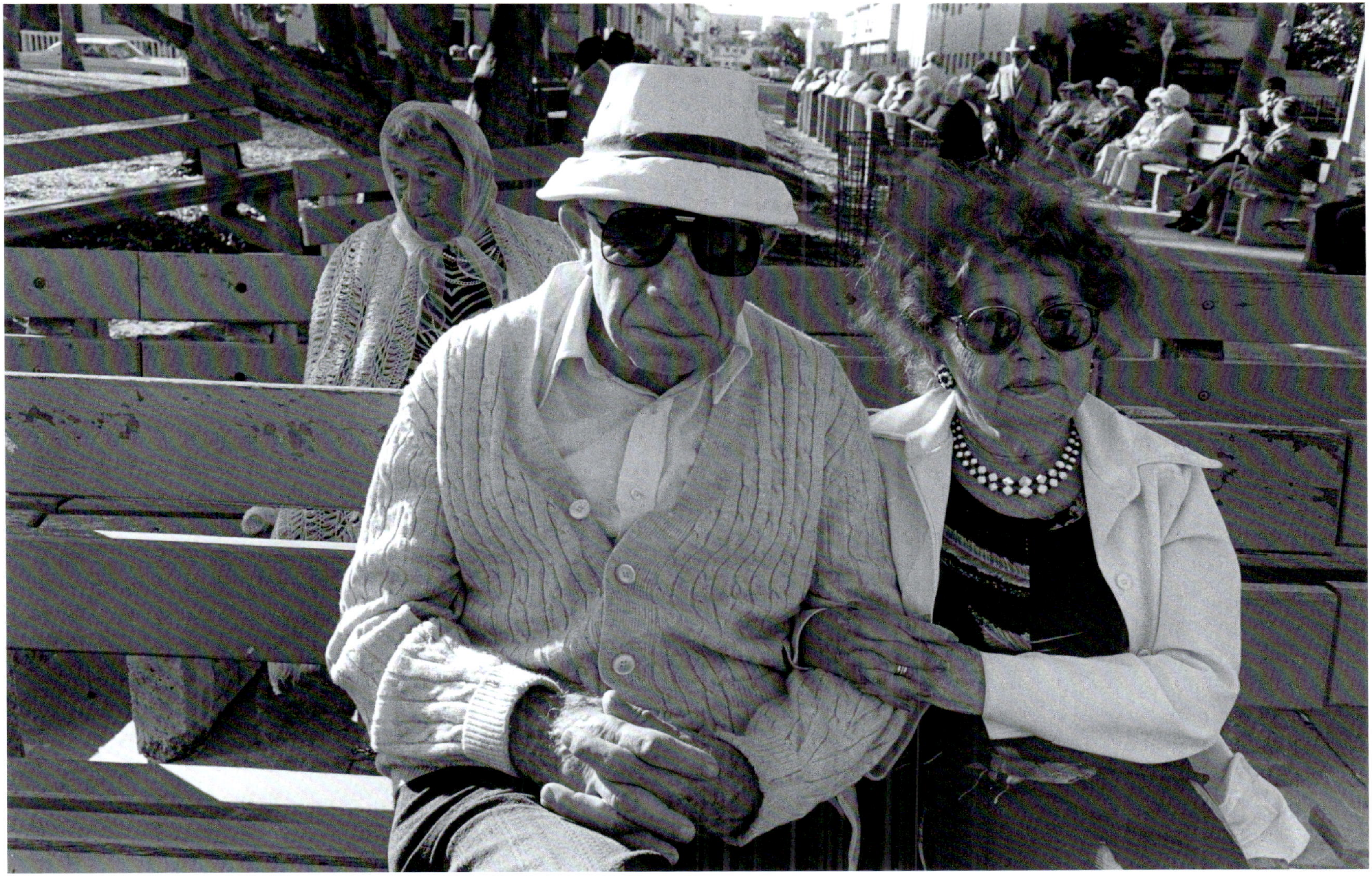

Men in succah, 1980

Men sit in a succah, a temporary hut used during the festival of Sukkot, at the An-Nell Hotel.

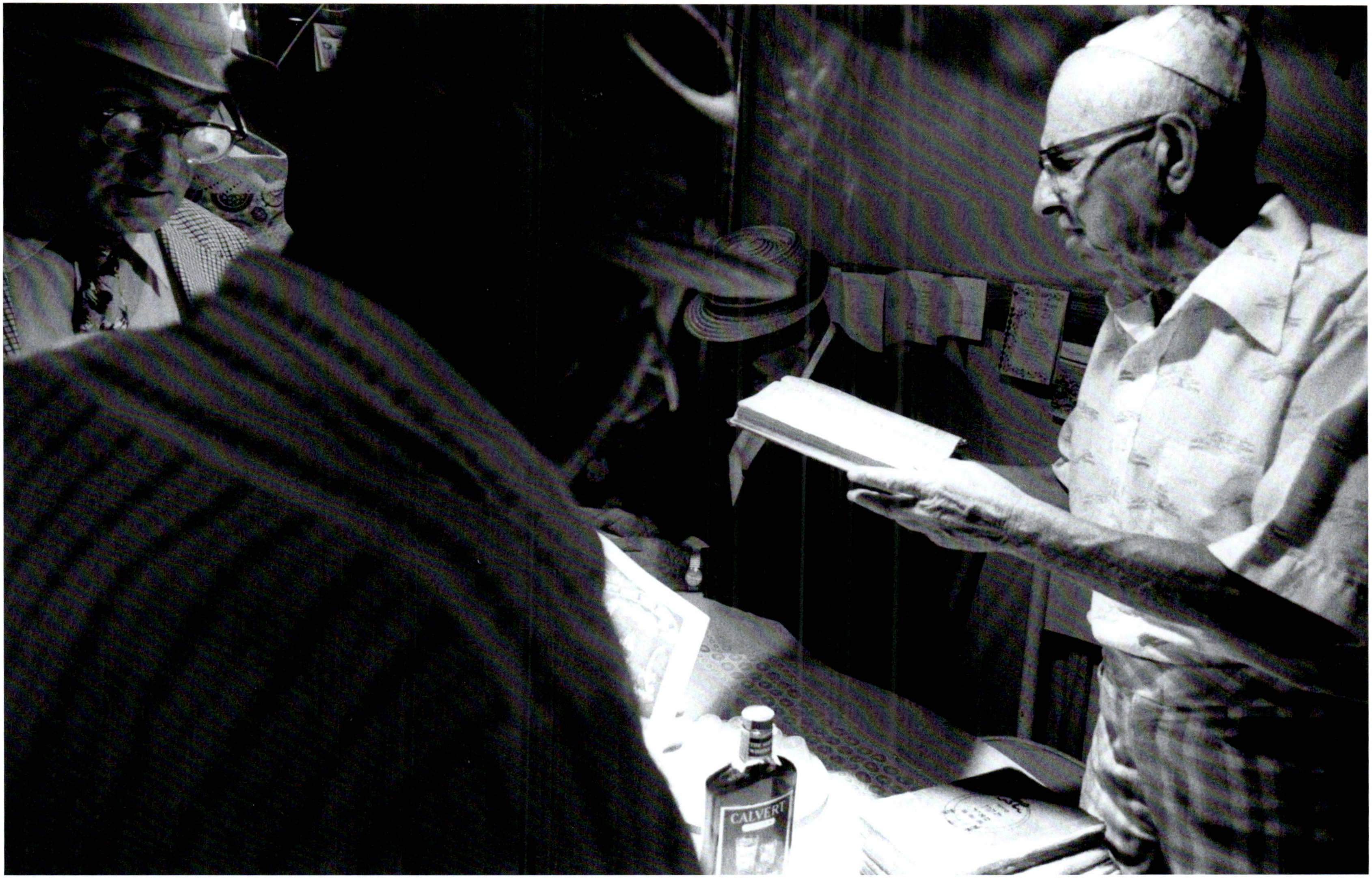
CALVERT

Lighting Shabbos candles, 1983

Orthodoxy requires that men and women pray separately. However, the fire marshal ordered that Shabbos candles, which are lit on sunset at Friday, the beginning of the weekly day of rest, not be lit in one's hotel room. So, these were lit communally.

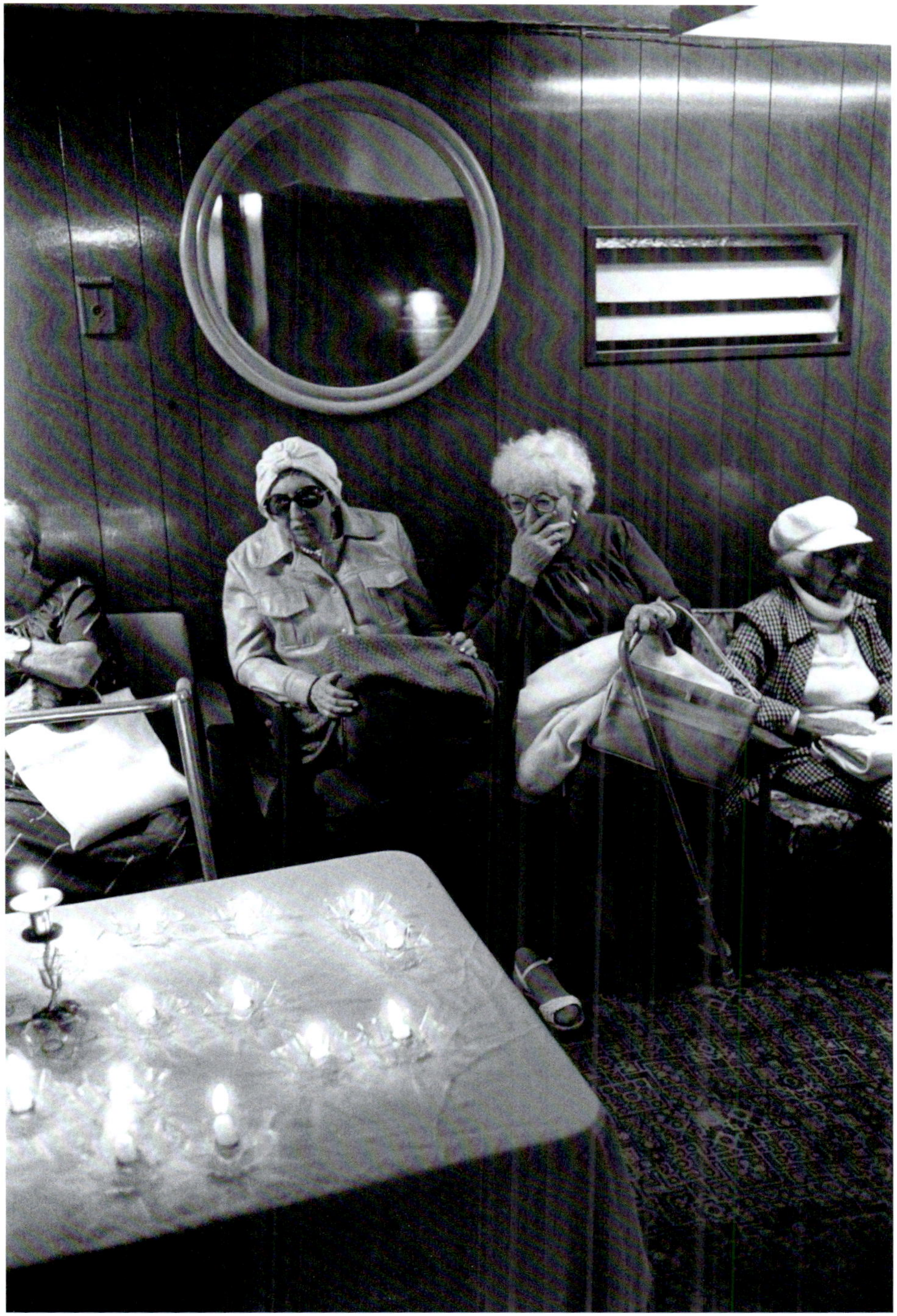

Passover Seder, 1980

People partake in a Seder dinner for the Passover holiday at the Blackstone Hotel.

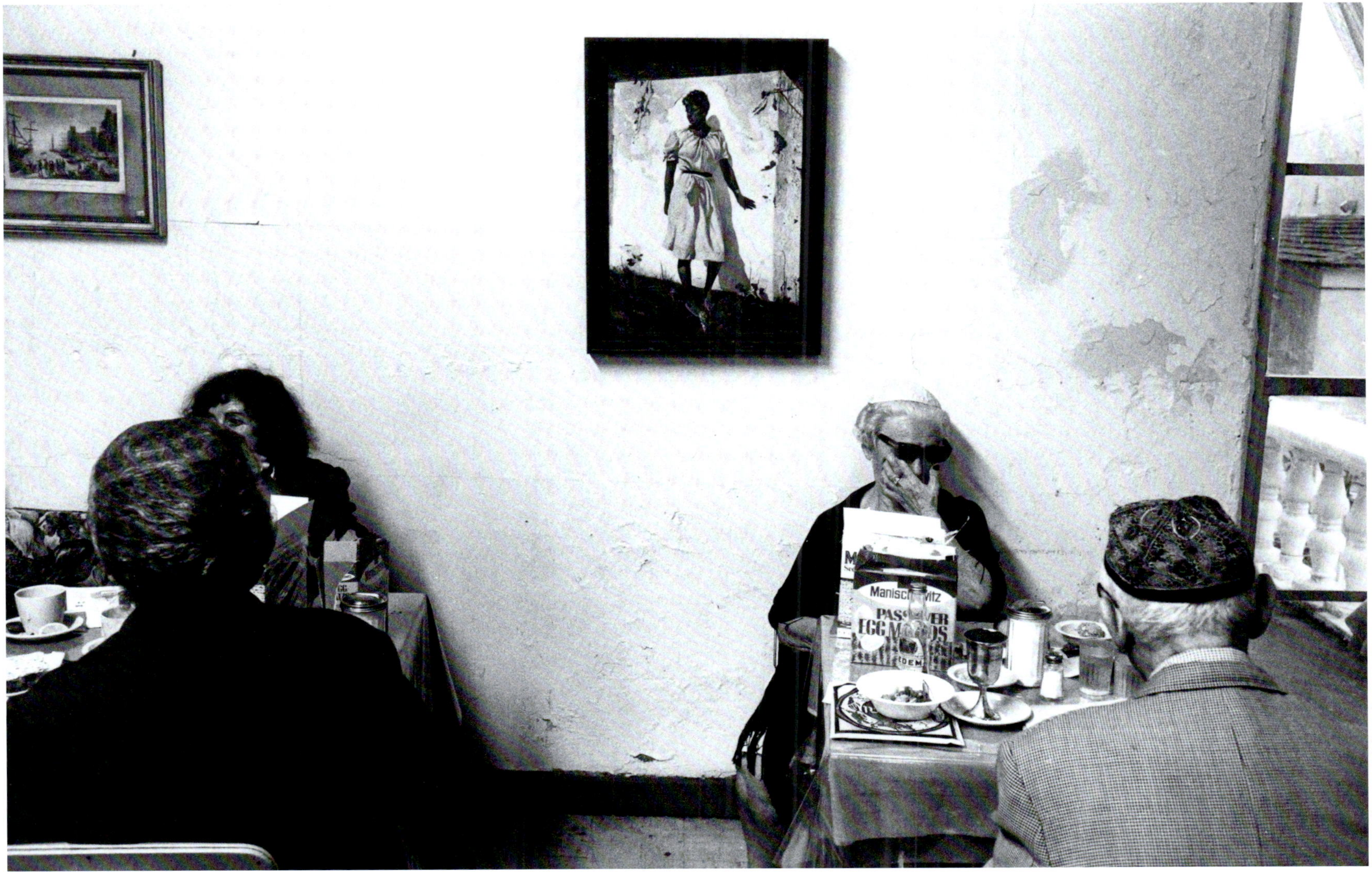

Man covering graven image, 1983

In a makeshift shul at the Tudor Hotel, an Orthodox man, deeming the framed graven image print not fitting for a place of worship, covers it before a Friday evening prayer service.

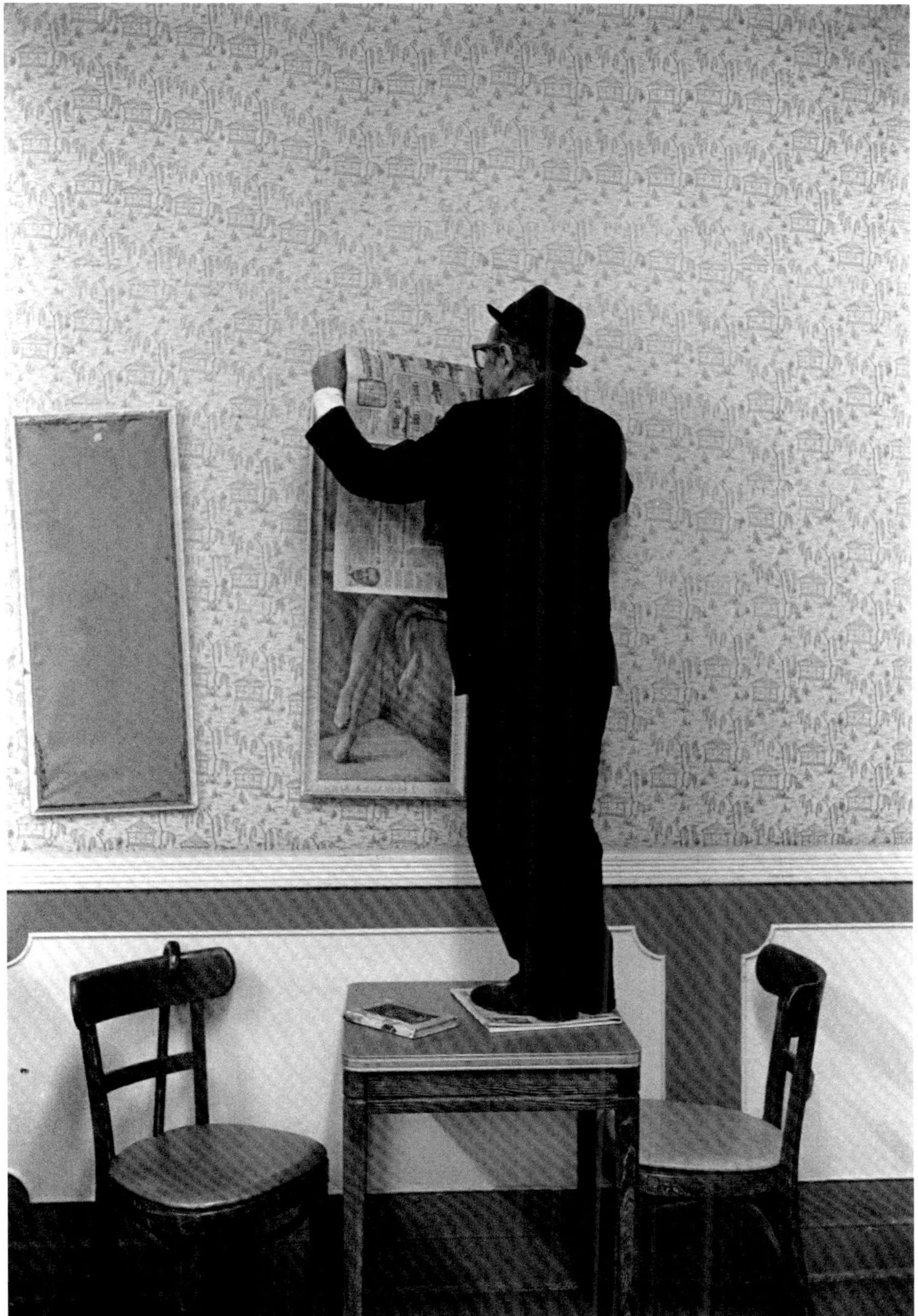

Hitler as the angel of death, 1977

A woman showing a painting of Hitler as the angel of death that hung in the living room of her apartment but was kept shrouded with a white bed sheet.

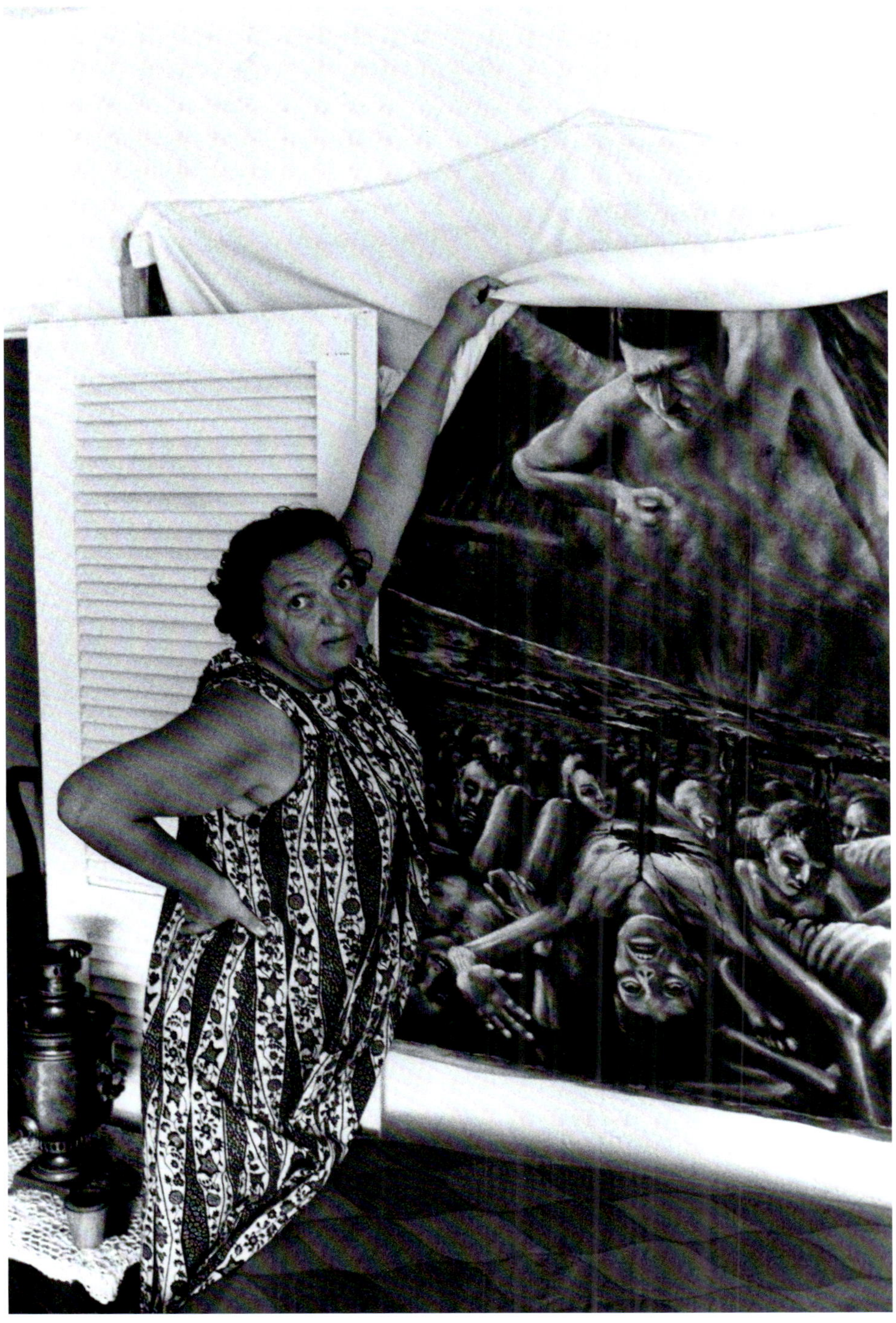

Couple watching television in a hotel lobby, 1984

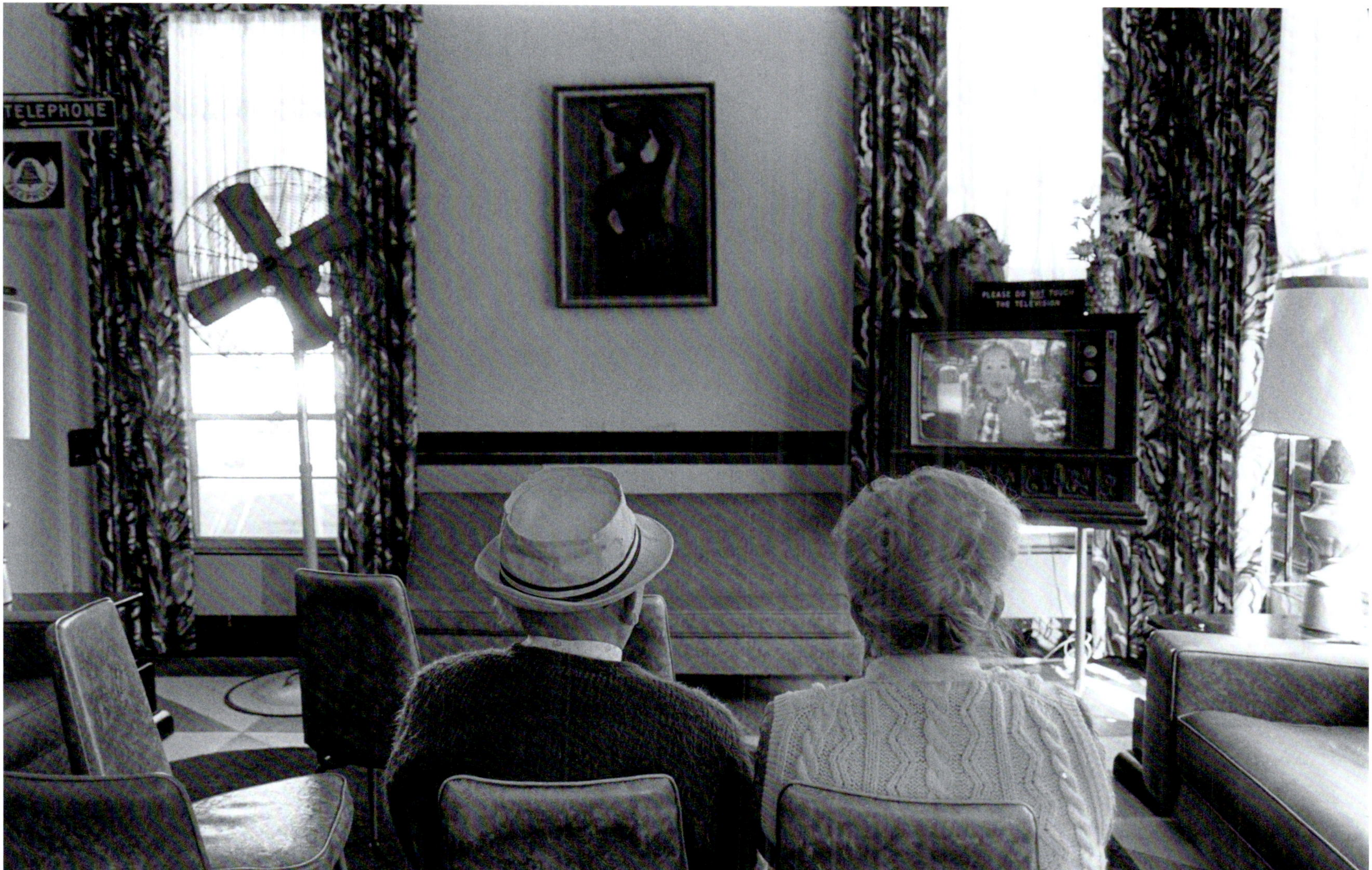
TELEPHONE
PLEASE DO NOT TOUCH
THE TELEVISION

Chess game, 1978

Orthodox men play chess in front of an Earl LePan mural. LePan painted murals in the latter 1930s in south Florida; a few remain in South Beach hotels.

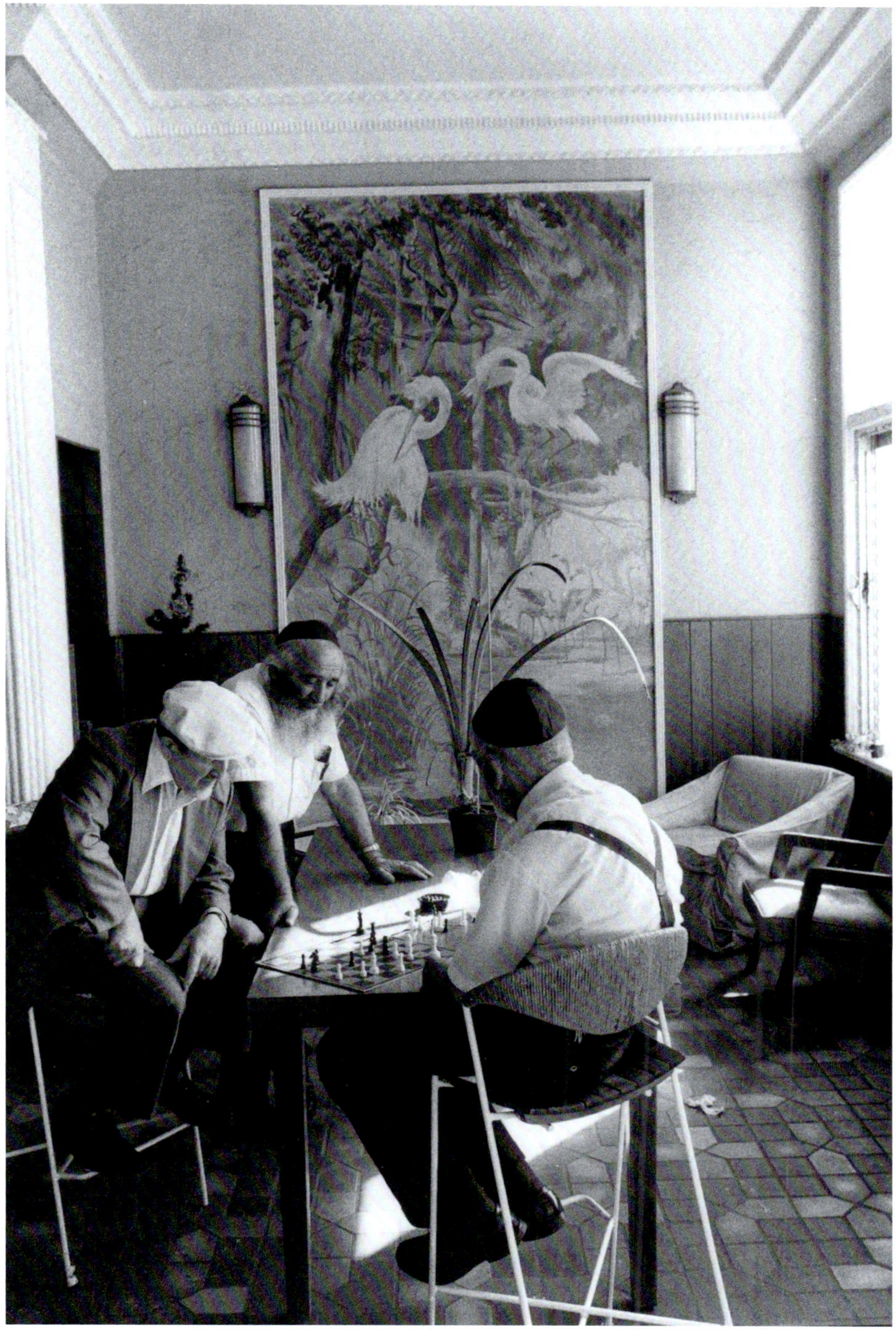

Hotel lobby, 1986

South Beach was a vibrant social place. Live vaudeville-type entertainment was offered at certain hotels. Social clubs abounded, while hotel lobbies were often used to meet and greet anybody at any time.

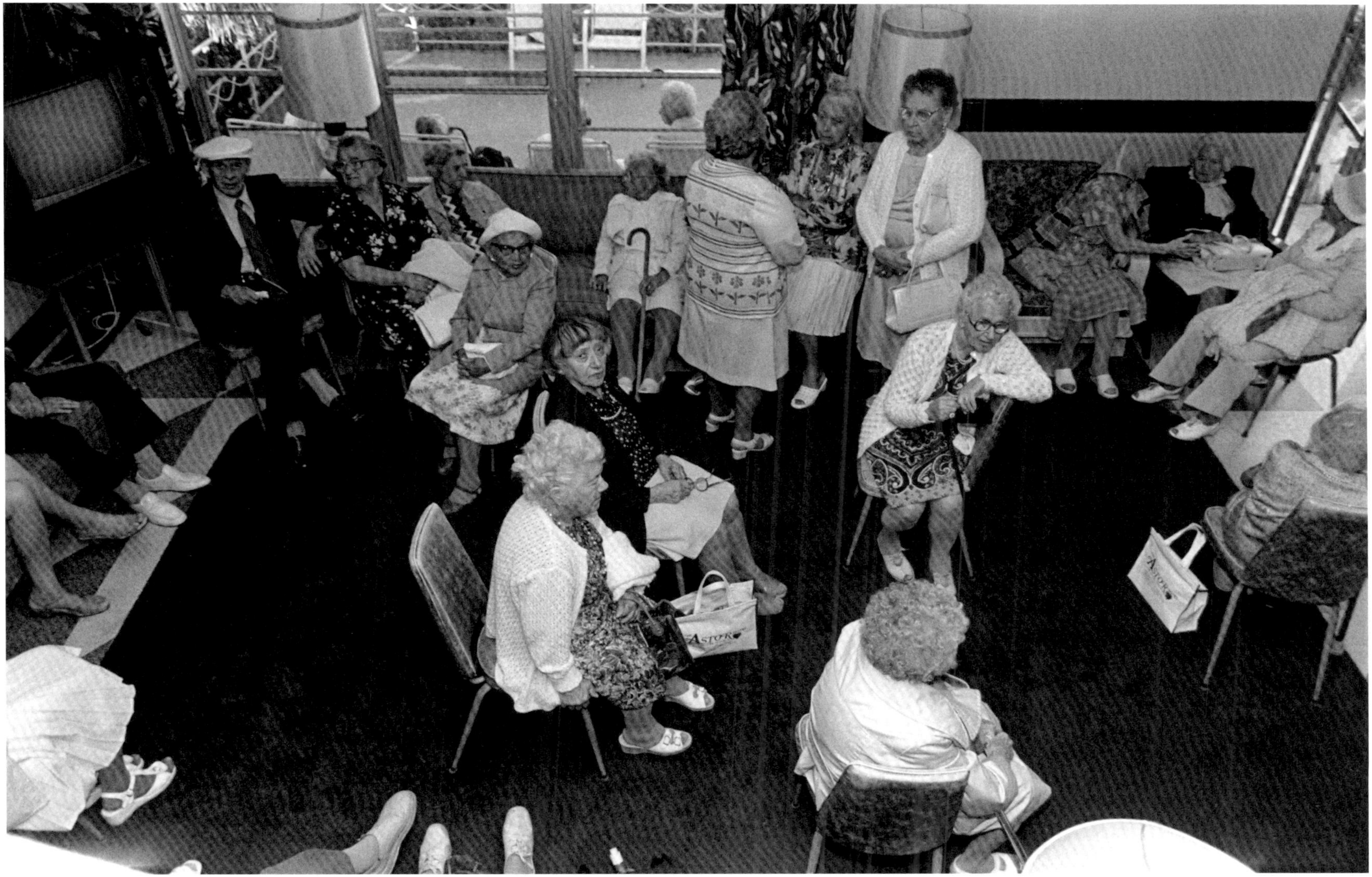
ASTOR
ASTOR

Boxed meals, 1980

Hot meals were served throughout the week at Tenth Street Auditorium. Meals were boxed and distributed in advance of holidays. A Meals-on-Wheels program delivered meals to the homebound.

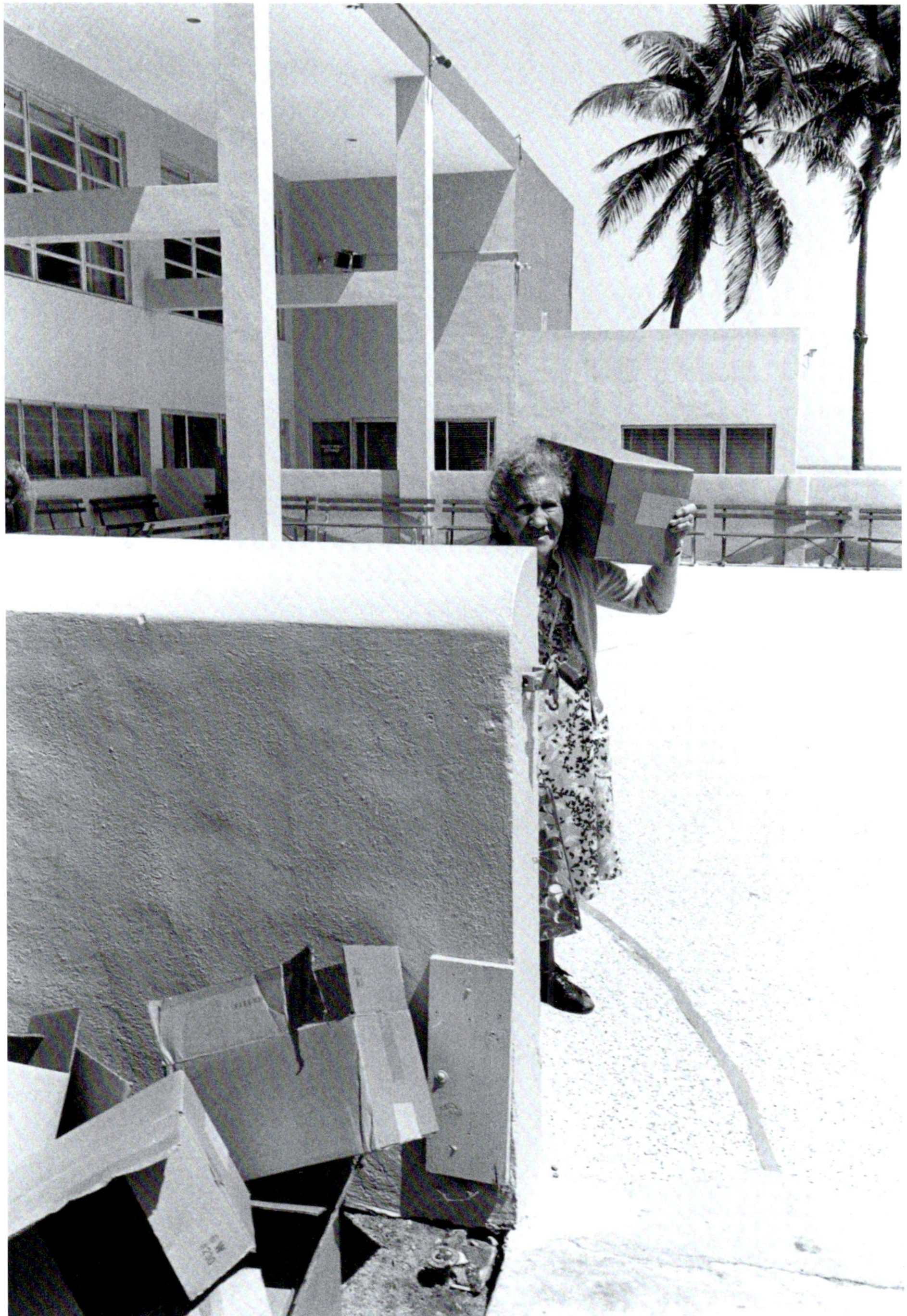

Man in hotel dining room, 1984

Some hotels offered meal plans, a leftover function from the more halcyon days of American-plan vacations to Miami Beach. Rooms were without kitchens, although some had kitchenettes.

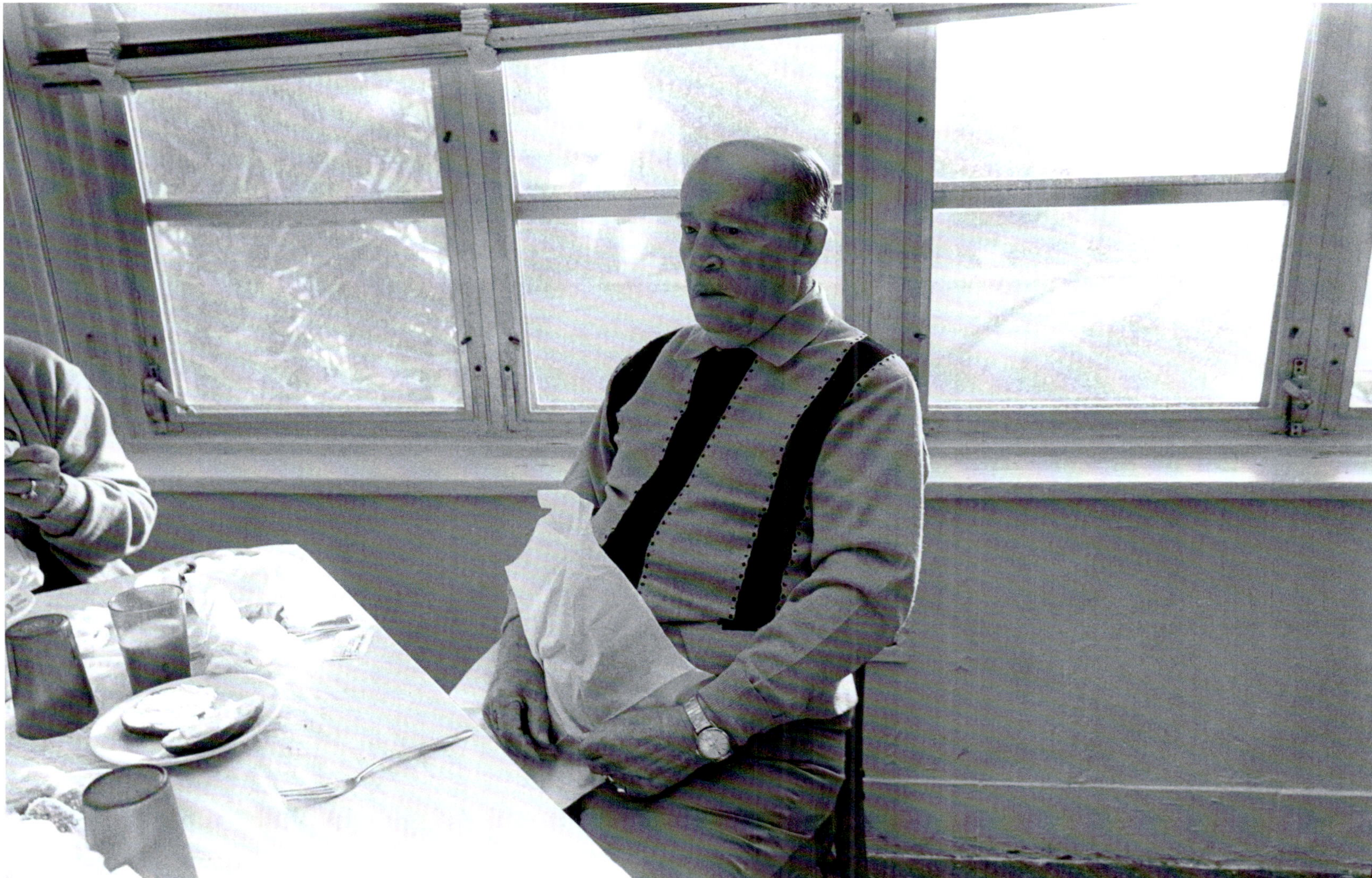

Woman in hotel dining room, 1984

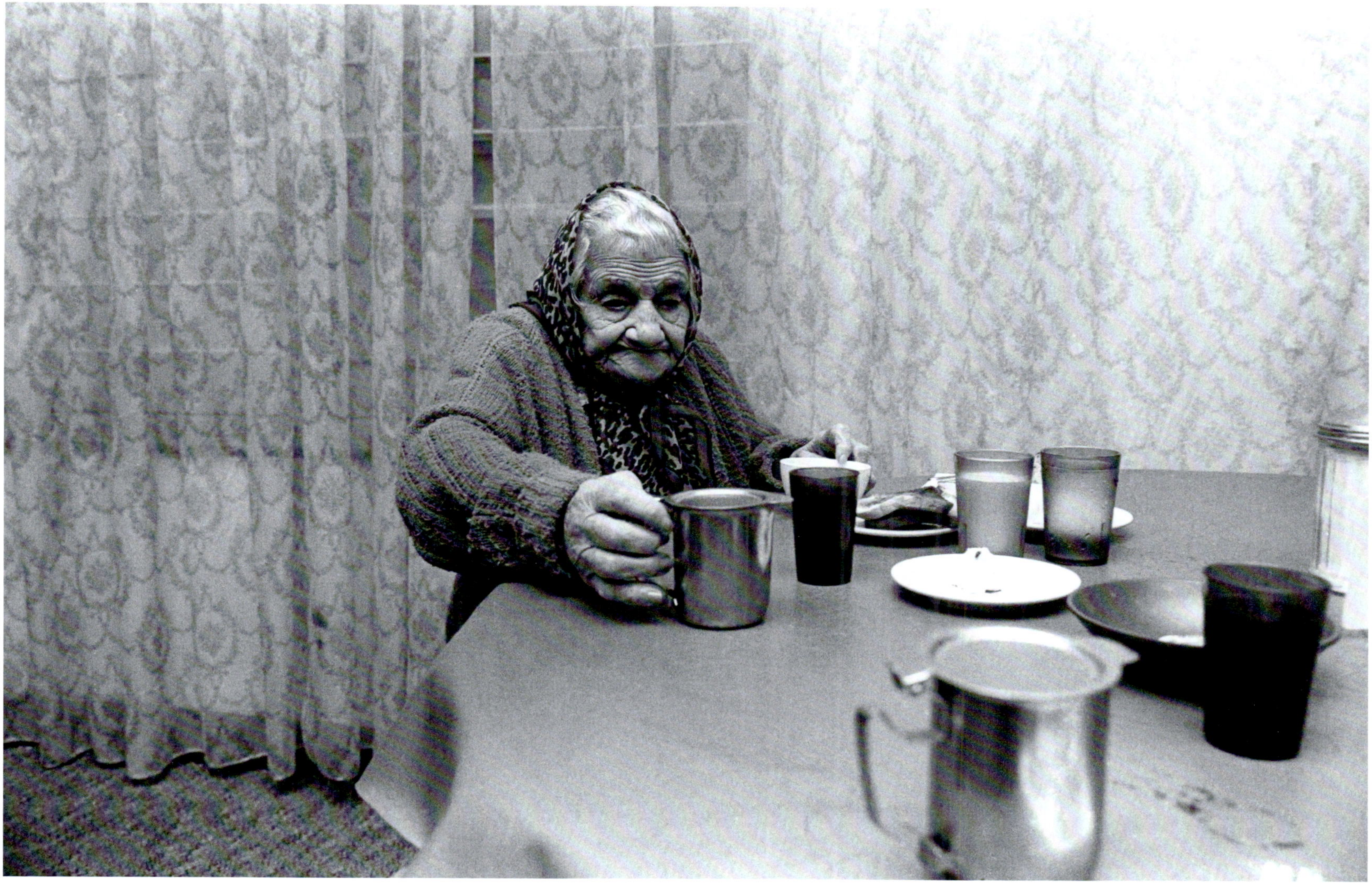

Woman in room, 1984

Sun, sand, and surf lured tourists to Miami Beach, and the few streets closest to the ocean were lined by small, mostly art deco–designed hotels. They offered refuge seasonally or yearly to an increasingly elderly clientele.

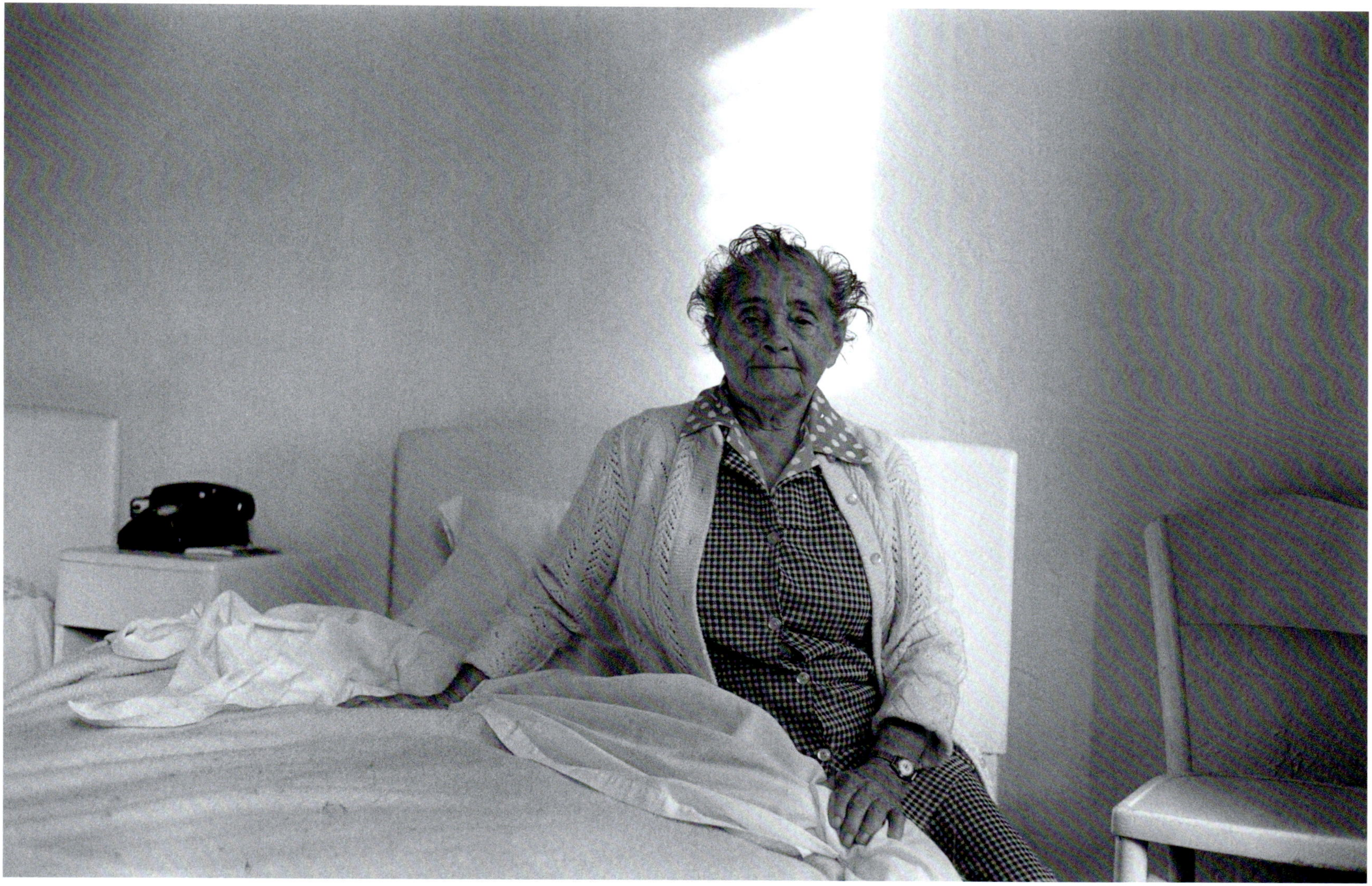

Woman in room, 1980

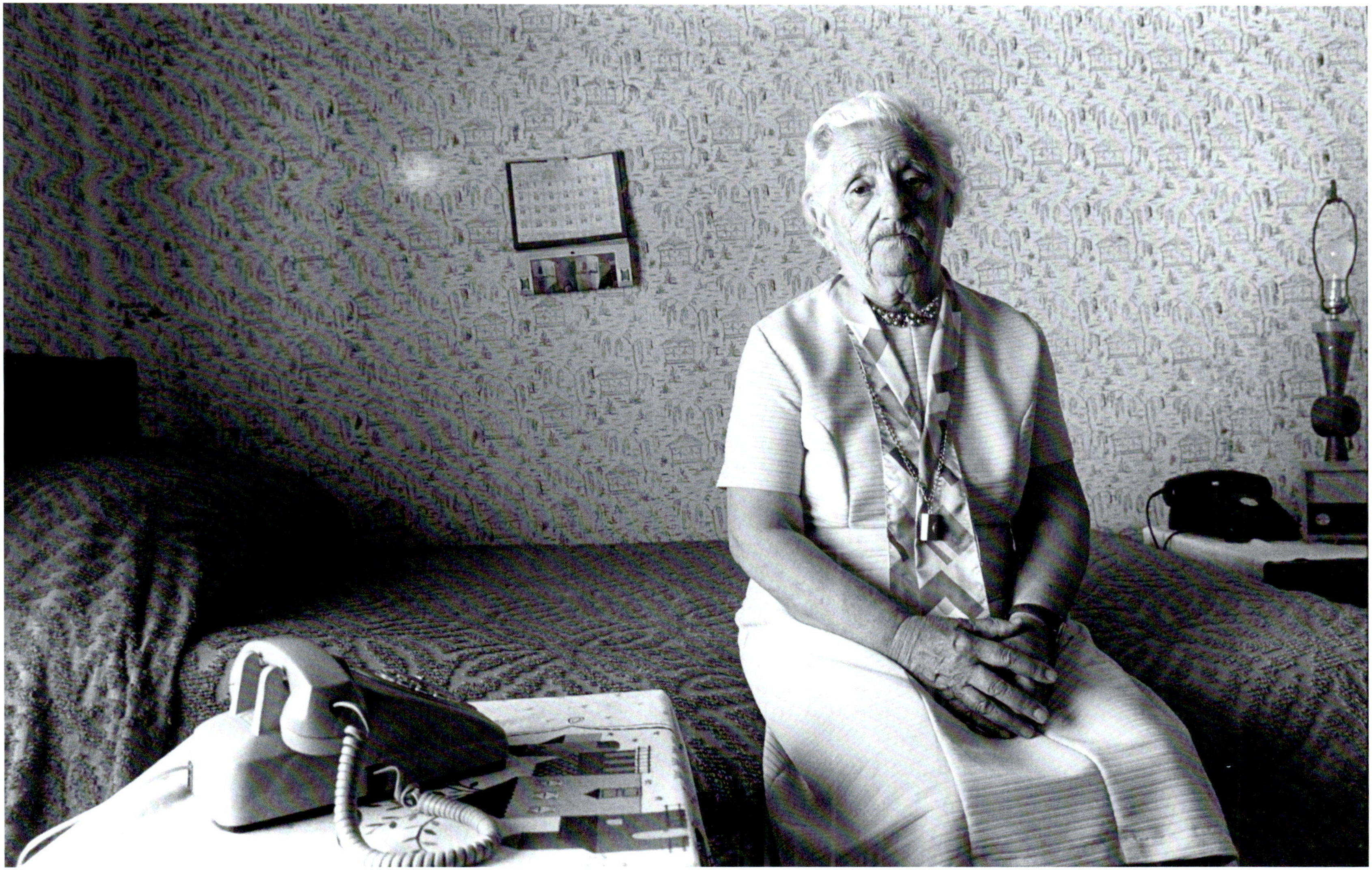

Woman in room, 1984

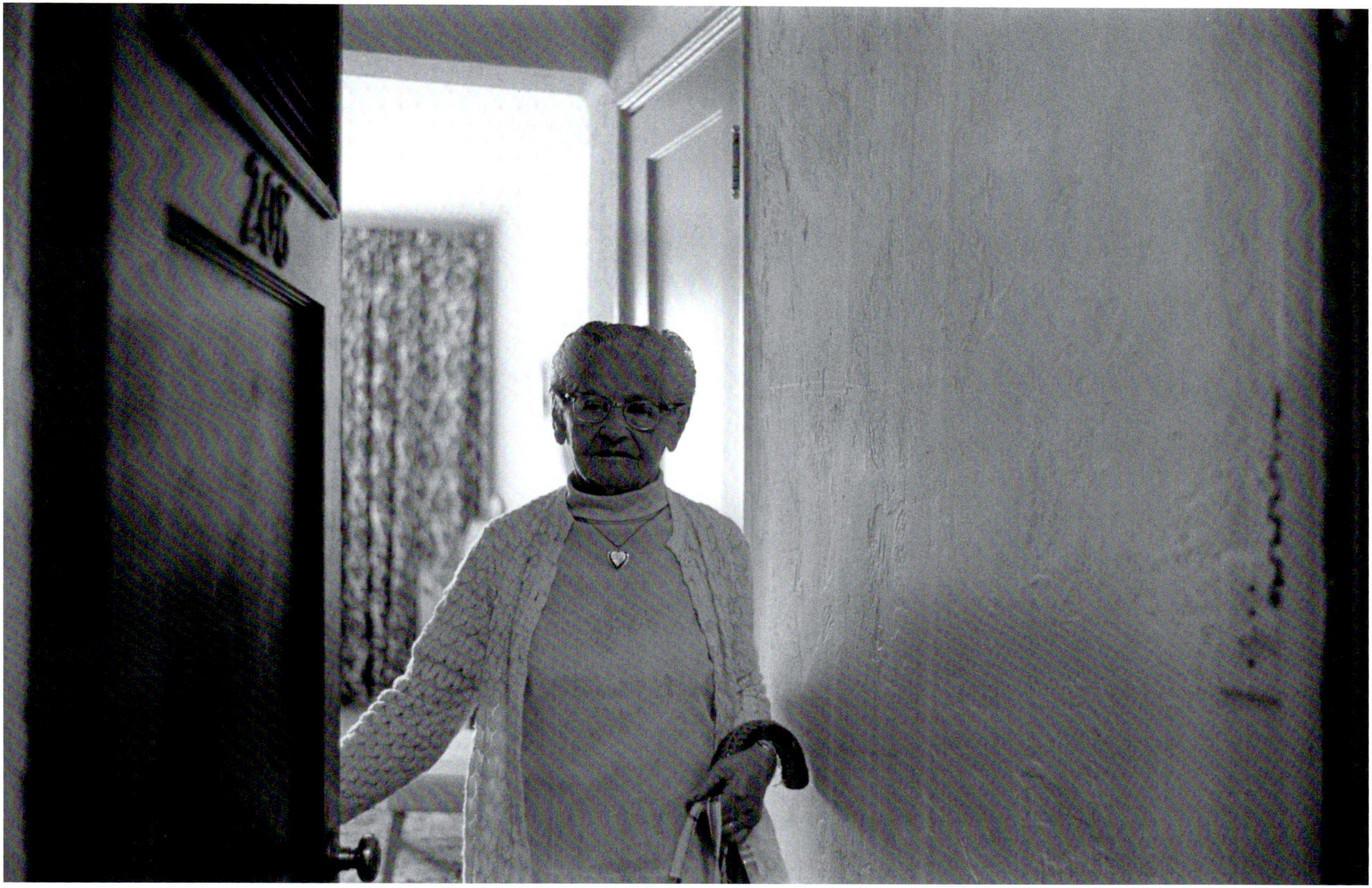

Woman in room, 1984

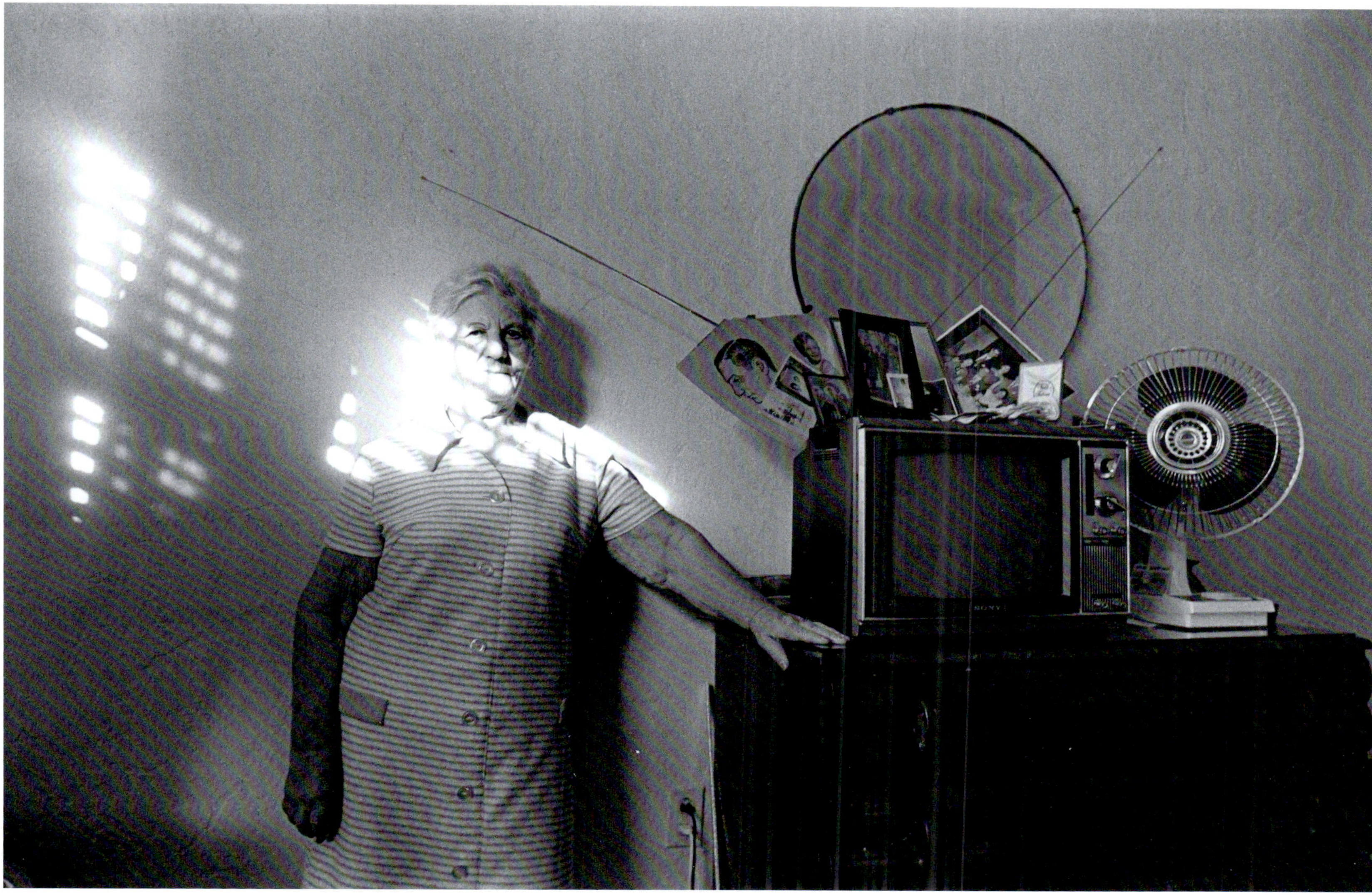

Man in room, 1984

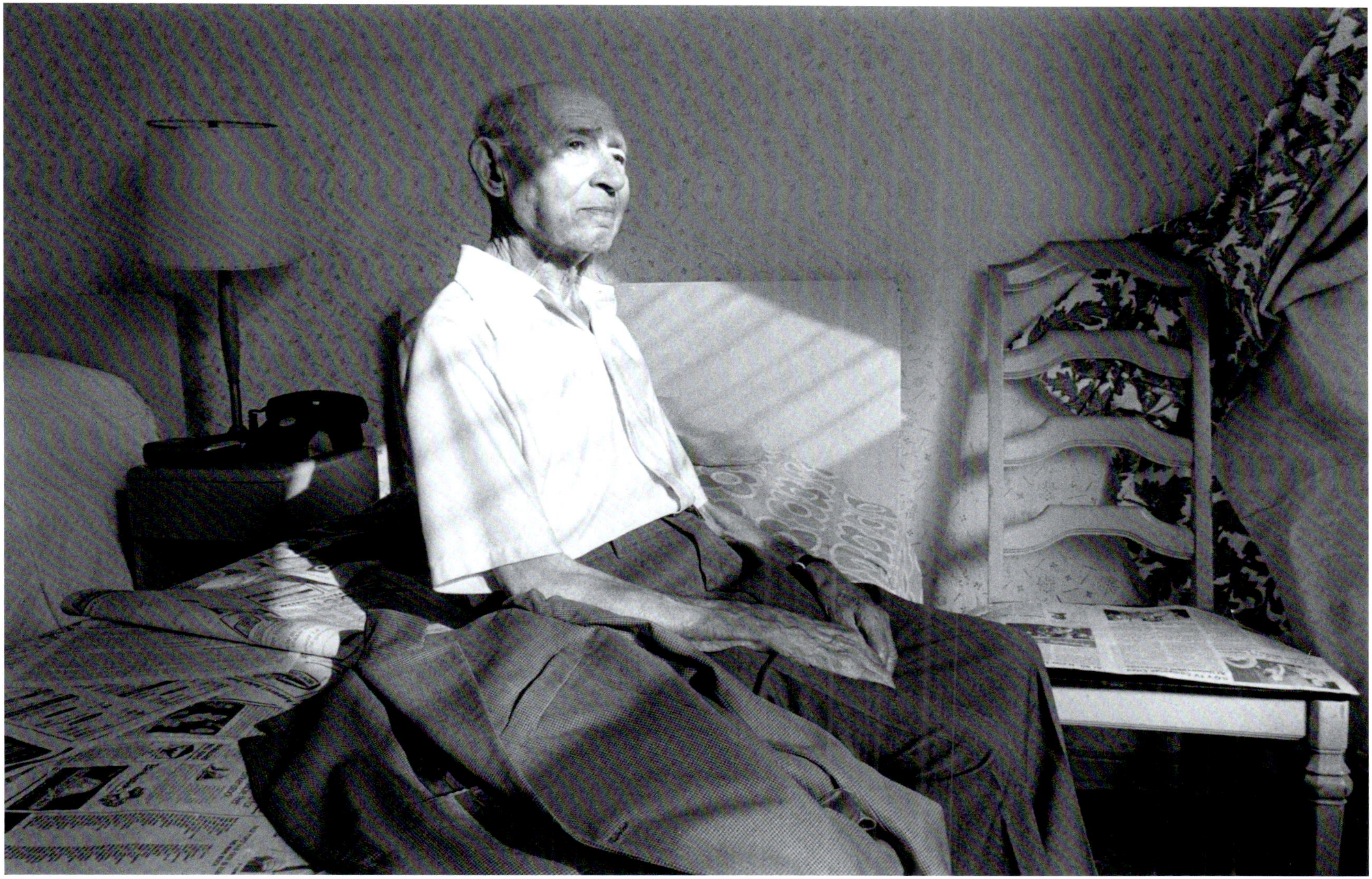

Man in room, 1984

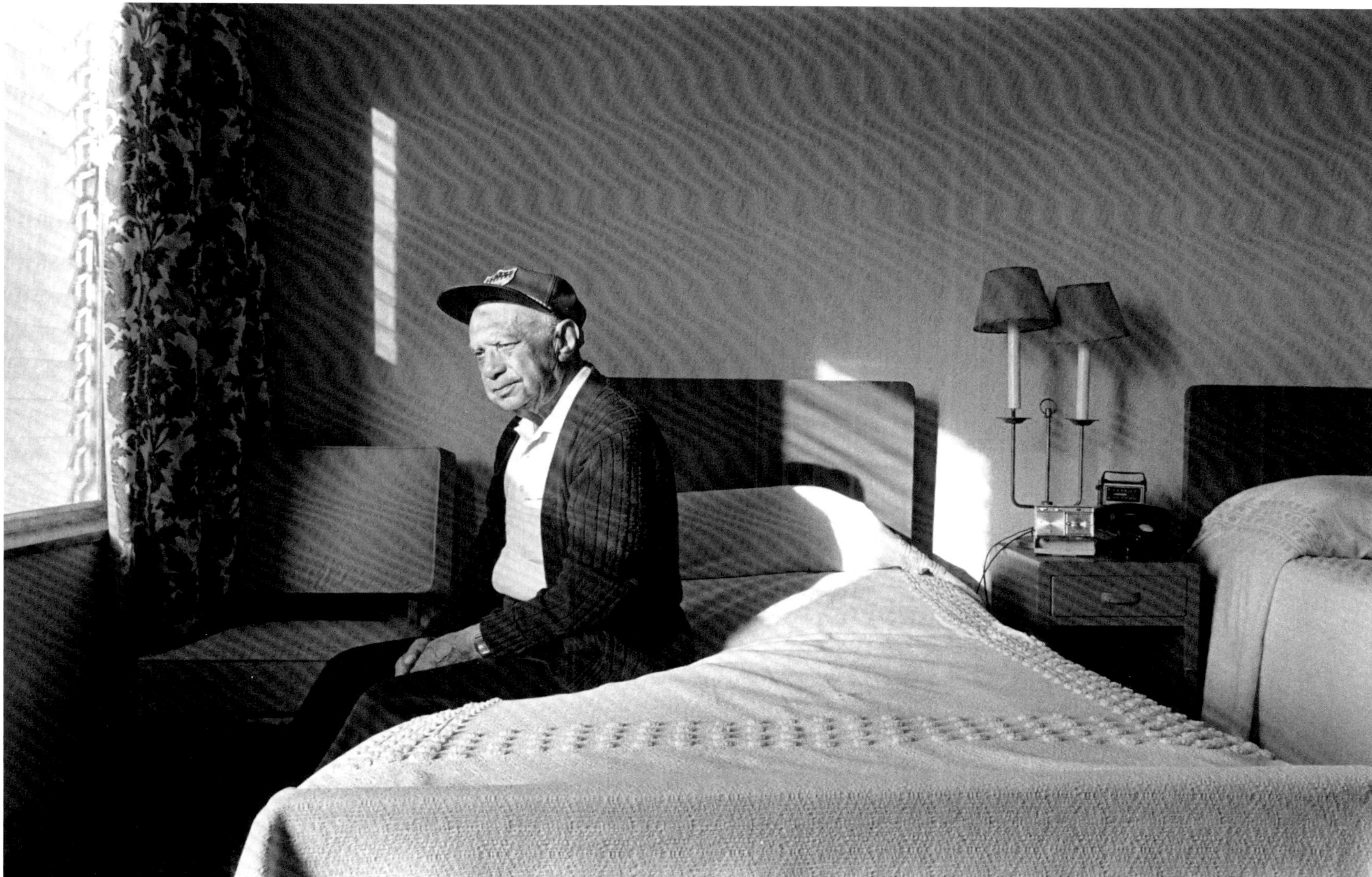

Man in room, 1980

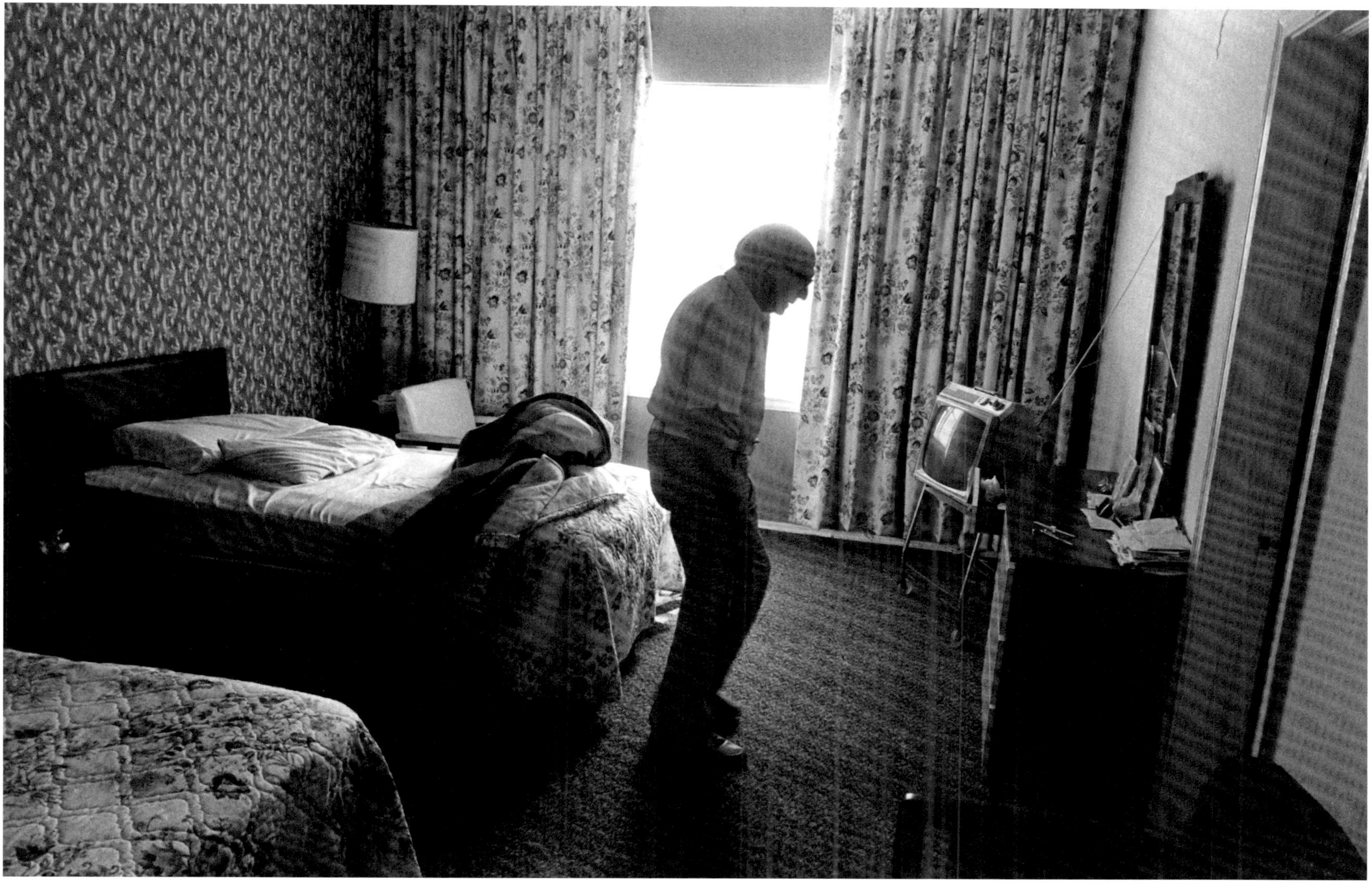

Woman mounting stairs in hotel, 1980

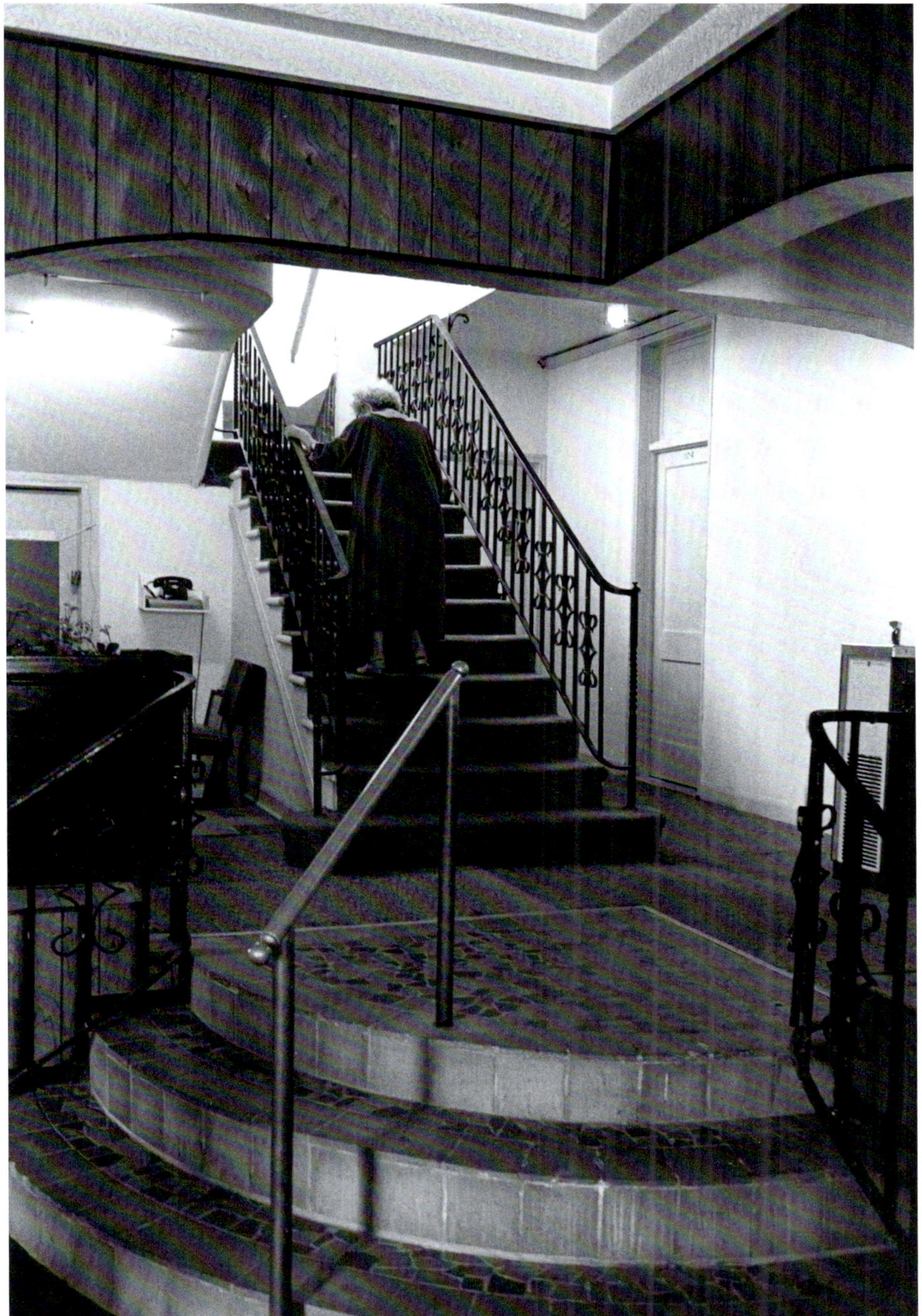

Round dance, 1977

Round dances were held weekly at Pier Park. The park was demolished long ago, along with the fishing pier. Women in South Beach outnumbered men.

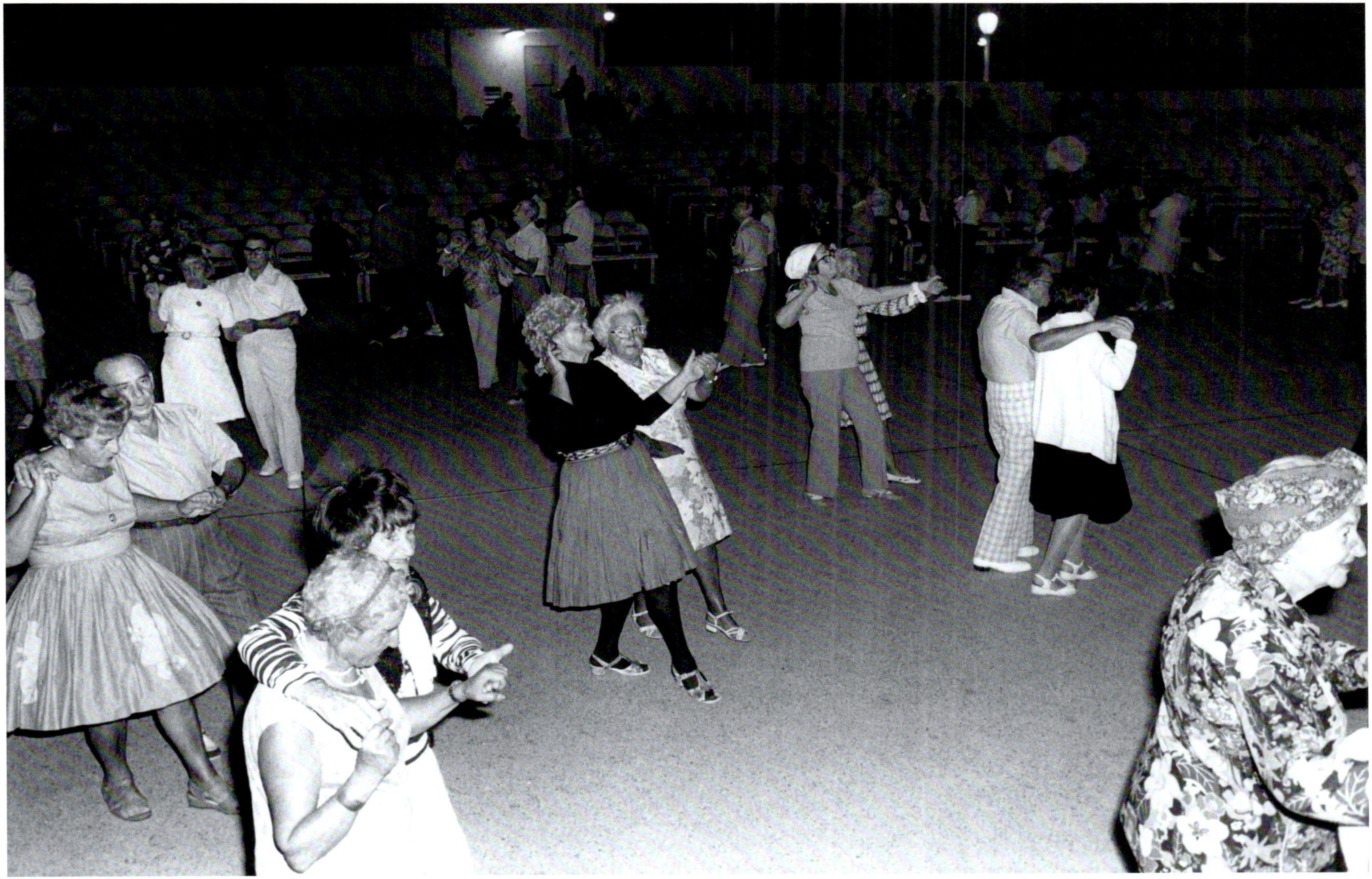

New Year's Eve party, 1978

These elderly people, who had seen and often endured too much, would greet both the days and the new year joyously, with optimism and a zest for life. Most hoteliers threw New Year's Eve parties for their guests, making South Beach especially lively that night of the year.

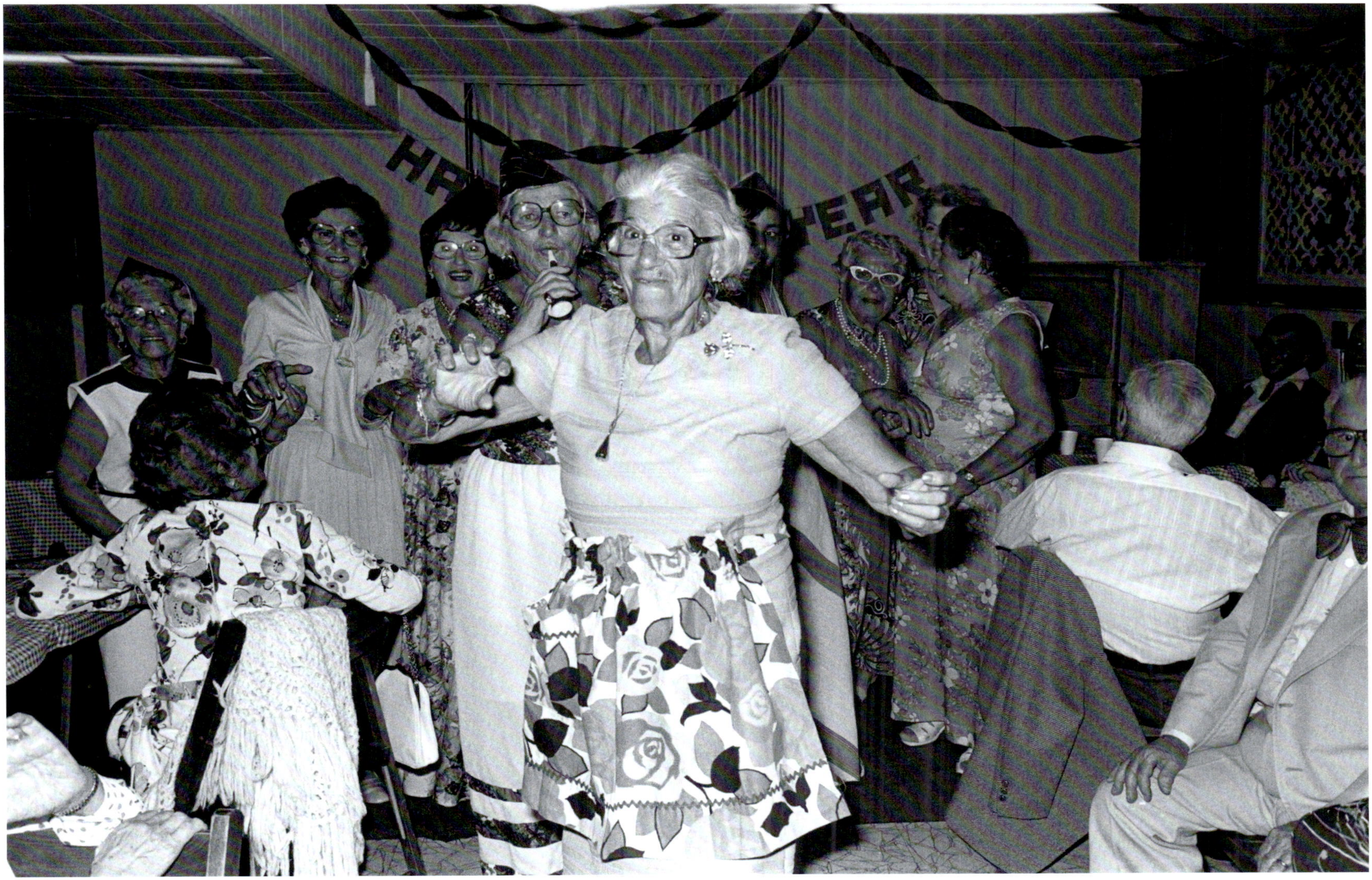

New Year's Eve party, 1978

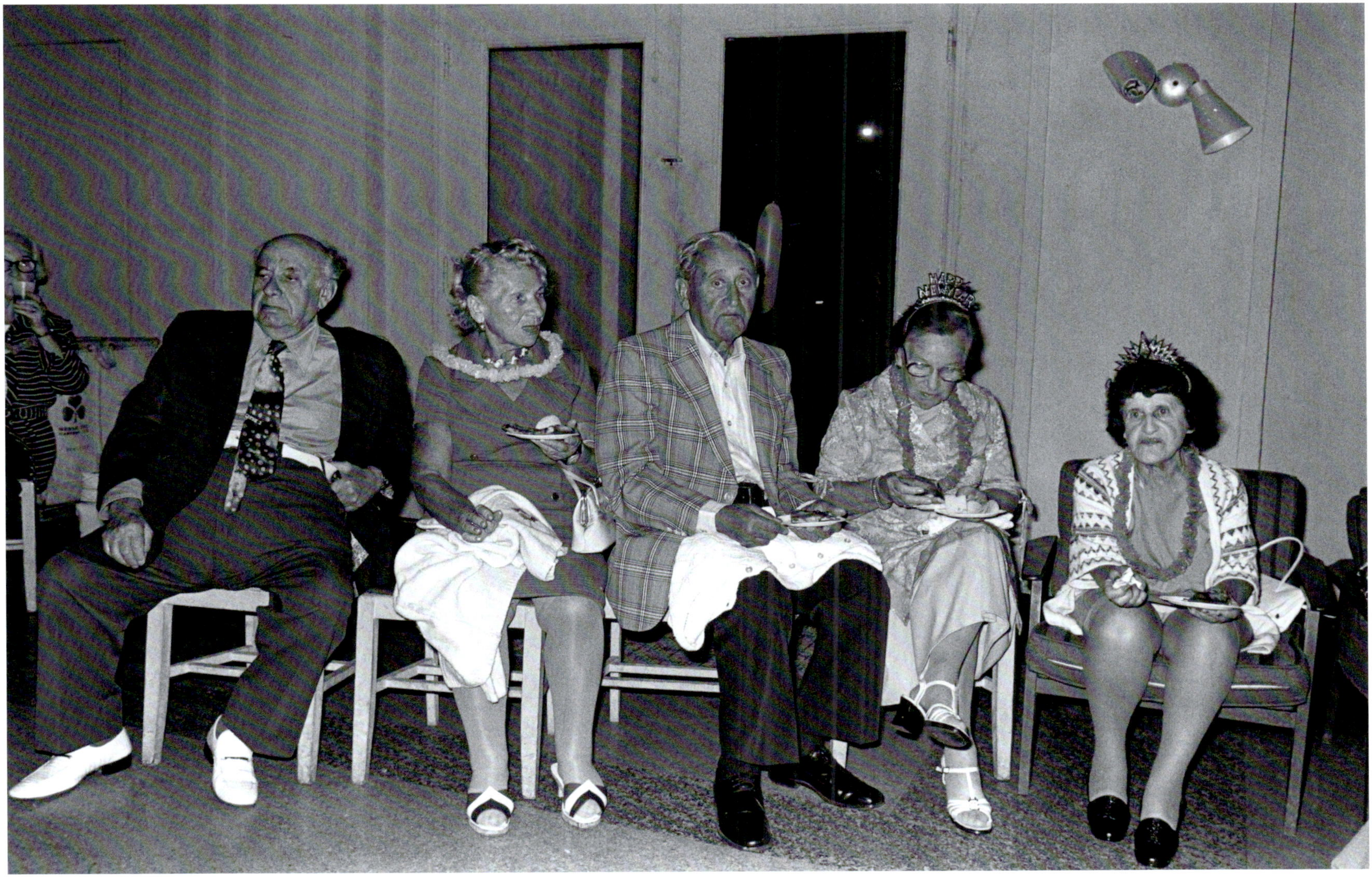

New Year's Eve party, 1983

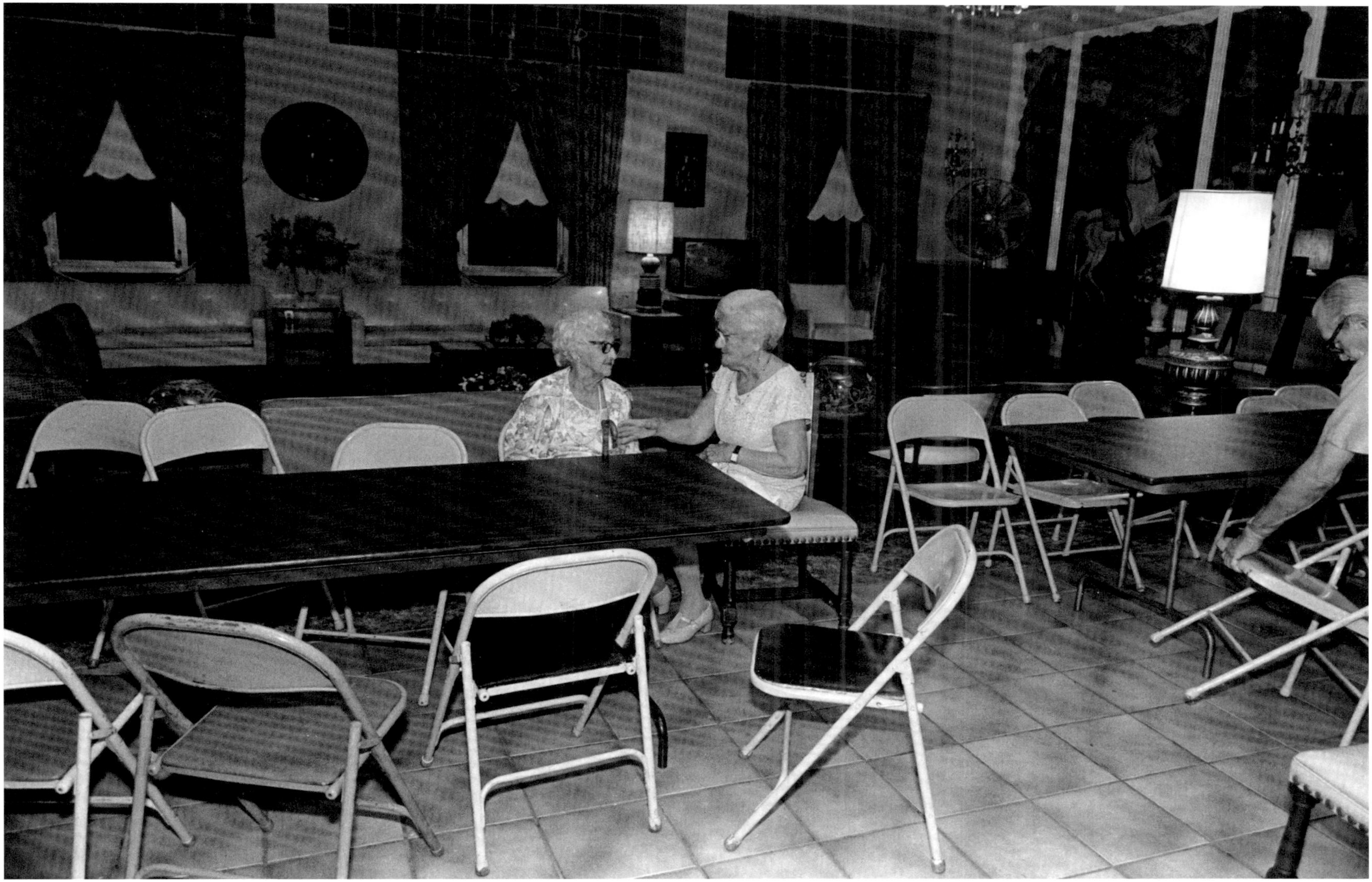

Women walking in hotel hallway, 1984

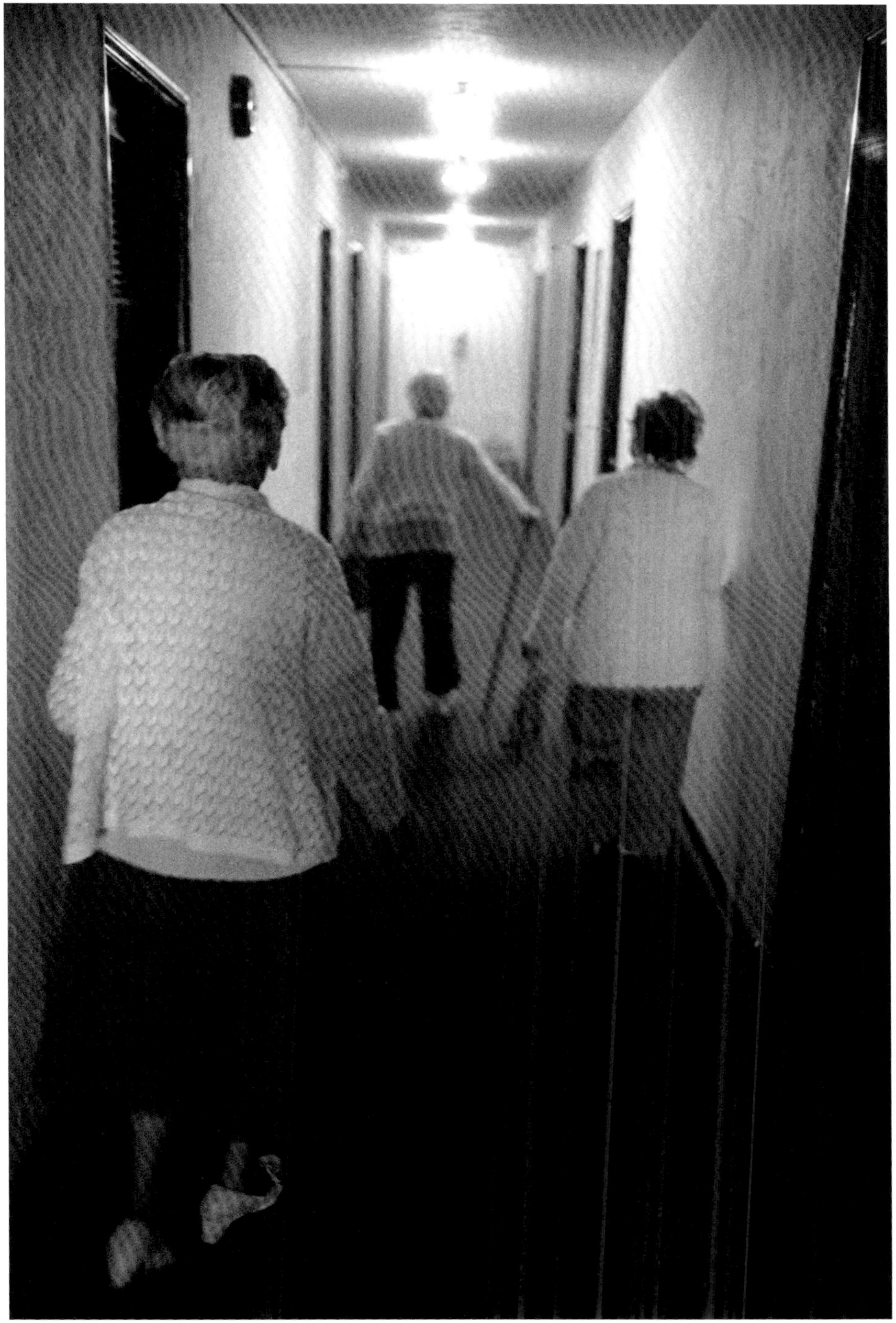

Gary Monroe, a native of Miami Beach, received a master's degree in fine arts from the University of Colorado at Boulder in 1977. For the next ten years, he photographed the old-world Jewish community that characterized Miami's South Beach. After encountering Haitian refugees in detention at the INS Krome Resettlement Camp, he made more than two dozen trips to Haiti, through 2000, compiling an array of photographs depicting life prior to the arrival of the mass media in the 1990s. Across Florida, Monroe trained his eye on vacationers at Disney World, the spiritualist community of Cassadaga, old Florida tourist attractions, and the phenomenon of increasing suburban development. Mr. Monroe has traveled globally to Brazil, Israel, Cuba, India, France, and Russia, while maintaining his curiosity about all things Florida.

Gary Monroe has received grants from the National Endowment for the Arts, Florida Department of State's Division of Cultural Affairs, Florida Humanities Council, and the Fulbright Foundation to support his photography. He continues to use a Leica M-4 camera and Tri-X film, from which he crafts gelatin silver prints.

Gary Monroe is the author of several books, including *The Highwaymen: Florida's African-American Landscape Painters* and *Silver Springs: The Underwater Photographs of Bruce Mozert*.